D0774958

HARRY BENSON
ON PHOTOJOURNALISM

HARRY BENSON
ON PHOTOJOURNALISM

Photographs by
Harry Benson

Text by
Gigi and Harry Benson

Harmony Books/New York

Acknowledgments

I would like to thank our publisher, Bruce Harris, Ken Sansone, our art director, and especially our editor, Manuela Soares, without all of whom this book would not have been published. My thanks also to Hanns Kohl for the black-and-white printing, Chris Christoupolos, Kate Guardino, and Joseph Randazzo from Time/Life, and to David Cairns and Philip Seltzer.

The majority of the photographs in this book were taken with the Minolta 35-mm system.

Pages 30–31 (Mrs. Betty Ford). Courtesy *Vogue.* Copyright © 1974 by The Condé Nast Publications Inc. Page 108 (Dennis Hopper and Peter Fonda). Courtesy *Vogue.* Copyright© 1969 by The Condé Nast Publications Inc. Page 102 (Paloma Picasso). Copyright © 1981 The Hearst Corporation. Courtesy of *Harper's Bazaar.* Page 46 ("Three's Company"). Courtesy *People* magazine. Copyright © Time, Inc. 1977. All rights reserved. Reprinted with permission. Pages 134–35 (Janet Tanner). Courtesy *Life* magazine. Copyright © Time, Inc. 1981. All rights reserved. Reprinted with permission.

Copyright © 1982 Gigi and Harry Benson
All rights reserved. No part of this book may be reproduced or transmitted in any form or by any means, electronic or mechanical, including photocopying, recording, or by any information storage and retrieval system, without permission in writing from the publisher.

Published by Harmony Books, a division of Crown Publishers, Inc., One Park Avenue, New York, New York 10016 and simultaneously in Canada by General Publishing Company Limited

HARMONY BOOKS and colophon are trademarks of Crown Publishers, Inc.

Manufactured in the United States of America

Library of Congress Cataloging in Publication Data

Benson, Harry.
     Harry Benson on photojournalism.

     1. Photography, Journalistic. I. Benson, Gigi. II. Title.
TR820.B425   1982   778.9′907   82-1005
ISBN: 0-517-544490   AACR2
ISBN: 0-517-544504 (pbk.)

Designed by Ken Sansone

10 9 8 7 6 5 4 3 2 1
First Edition

To
Wendy and Tessa
and
to my parents

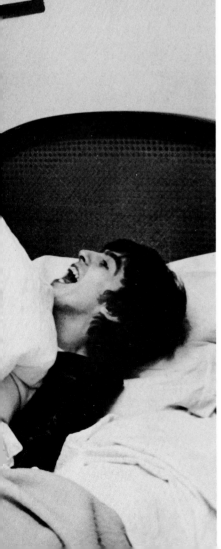

CONTENTS

STARTING OUT

I recall the first photograph to have an impact on me, the first time I was moved or touched by a picture on a page. I couldn't have been more than five or six at the time. It was a photograph that appeared in the *Glasgow Bulletin* of a little baby crying beside some wreckage. It is a famous picture and has stuck with me for years. That is what a good photograph should do—provoke a response, make you remember it.

A good photograph is obvious: everything fits, everything is balanced. You just want to look at it. All great photos have an edge to them, a certain amount of drama; they hold your interest and start you thinking. The bottom line is always subjective, though—it comes down to whether or not you like them when you see them on a page.

My main purpose as a photojournalist is to bring back the pictures—at least one good one from each assignment. The margin between success and failure in photography is as slim as a dog's whisker. I have found that if I work hard, trust my instincts, and let my imagination go, I'm likely to get lucky. If I don't come back with one good picture I feel the assignment was a terrible waste of time. I missed the picture that I'm sure was there.

I grew up in Glasgow during the war, and the crisis and drama that were my everyday life made a lasting impression. Listening to Winston Churchill's speeches about the deeds of heroic men fighting great battles, I thought how exciting it would be to be a part of this, to participate in it. I began to want to get to the center of things, to see for myself what was going on. I began to visualize the drama, what it should look like.

My father gave me a box camera for Christmas when I was eleven years old, and I started taking pictures. I took it with me wherever I went and photographed whatever I thought was interesting. My first picture was published when I was sixteen. It was a picture of a roe deer in my father's zoo, taken with a Thornton Pickard 4 × 5 plate camera. I gave it to the *Glasgow Evening Times.* I looked and looked for it to appear, and then I gave up hope. About three months later, I got on a train in Glasgow. The man sitting next to me turned to the center spread and there was the picture. I wanted to shout, "It's mine! It's mine!" I bought a copy of the paper and sat and looked at the photograph for hours. To this day, I can't remember if they paid me for it, but that wasn't important. Seeing the picture in print was what mattered. That feeling has never left me.

I spent two years at the Glasgow School of Art, then served in the Royal Air Force. After that I played professional soccer in Glasgow while trying to get started as a photographer. I used to get up at 4:30 A.M. on Saturday and take the bus around Glasgow to photograph Catholic early Mass weddings in the morning, rush home to develop and print the pictures, and hurry back to the wedding receptions to try to get orders for pictures.

When I did get the opportunity to show picture editors my photographs, the pictures seemed to look ordinary and insignificant to me. When I tried to get a job at the *Glasgow Evening Citizen,* the picture editor told me I should be feeding animals in my father's zoo. (My father had founded the Calder Park Zoo in Glasgow.) I left almost in tears. For a few hours afterward I wondered if I had chosen the right profession or if I had the talent. Determined to show them all, I decided, "Photography is my life and I will stick to it."

I was hired by a local picture agency to cover the Loch Lomond area, doing mostly weddings. Then I was a staff photographer at a holiday camp, in 1951, where I photographed knobby-knee contests and sack races. It wasn't the best professional training, but it was a good way to meet girls.

My first newspaper job was with the *Hamilton Advertiser,* the largest weekly newspaper in Scotland, and the paper to which explorer David Livingston, a local boy from nearby Blantyre, sent his dispatches from Africa. Working for the *Advertiser* gave me discipline and purpose, because I knew my pictures were going to be published. Nearly four years at the *Advertiser* under editor Tom Murray was the equivalent of a university education, but I didn't need a degree. Like any photographer, I was as good as my pictures.

On my days off I occasionally took the train to London, going around Fleet Street trying to get a job. In Britain, if you've any interest in photojournalism at all, the place to be is Fleet Street, between the Old City and the West End, where all the national newspaper offices are located. Fleet Street is very chummy but extremely competitive. The photographers meet in pubs, gossip, talk about stories, and wait for the first editions of the papers to come out. They turn to their own papers first, to see how their pictures look; then they look at what the opposition has, to see if they just might have been beaten on a story.

It is a particular way of life, with an atmosphere of intrigue that is unique to Fleet Street; it doesn't exist in American journalism. The competition between the dailies is intense, and I've yet to see as much secrecy as surrounds an assignment anywhere else. There are secret meetings in pubs to plan how to scoop other papers, and dirty tricks to outdo your colleagues. It's good training for a photojournalist. I loved it.

On my seventh trip to London, I finally got to see the assistant picture editor of the London *Daily Sketch,* Freddy Wackett. He said there was the possibility of an opening for a free-lance photographer to cover Scotland. When I asked if there was a chance that I could do it, he looked up from his desk and gave a slight nod.

As a free-lance I would get paid only for stories that I did, not as a full-time employee, but to me getting a job on the *Daily Sketch* was the ultimate. It was highly regarded at that time as the newspaper with the best ideas on Fleet Street. It had good, hard-digging investigative reporters and photographers.

On one early assignment I went up to Balmoral Castle in Scotland to photograph the queen. Her little dog was running around barking, and the queen came out and said, "Well, Mr. Benson, what can I do for you today?" I just stuttered and stood there smiling, completely overawed at being spoken to by the queen. I got no pictures to speak of. I think it's impossible for an inexperienced photographer to go in and get good pictures in a situation like that, where you have only a little time with someone like the queen of England.

The biggest scare I ever got came from one of my first assignments for the *Daily Sketch.* An earl, one of the landed gentry in the border country in Scotland, had caught a poacher fishing on his private river. He shot the poacher in the backside and proceeded to march him for miles to the gamekeeper's lodge. The poacher nearly bled to death, and there was a big uproar about the case in court. To everyone's pleasure, His Lordship was charged and convicted. My reporter was in court, but I wasn't. I should have gone inside for at least a second, to see what the poacher looked like, but I relied on my reporter to point him out to me as they were leaving the court after the trial. As it turned out, my reporter pointed out the poacher's lawyer instead of the poacher.

My picture appeared on the front page of the *Sketch* the next day. I felt great until a phone call came from London, asking if I was happy. I said yes, very, and they said, "Well, stop being so happy, because the poacher's lawyer has been on to us and is going to sue. He wants some sort of satisfaction." I was devastated to have made such a terrible blunder when I was just starting out! I couldn't put the blame on the reporter; even though he had misled me, it was still my fault. I should have made absolutely sure. Luckily, the lawyer was not unreasonable, and it was all handled amicably.

I was doubly careful after that. I've never forgotten it. Now I'm glad it happened at the beginning of my career, because it made me very careful about identification. As the adage says, "When in doubt, leave it out."

After that things went more smoothly. I was doing very well for the *Sketch* in Glasgow. I could go where I wanted and suggest any story I wanted. When I won a prize in the Encyclopaedia Britannica awards, tying for second in the British Press Photographer of the Year competition, the *Sketch* asked me to come to London. So I went to London and was put on staff.

When you arrive in Fleet Street you are not welcomed with open arms: you have to serve an apprenticeship. I had thought things were tough in Glasgow, but I wasn't prepared for Fleet Street. A newcomer is considered a bit of an upstart, and treated accordingly. For instance, if there is a society meeting or a royal wedding or something happening outside 10 Downing Street, he could get there at six in the morning for an eleven o'clock photograph, but that doesn't mean he'll get the best position. A photographer who has been working for, say, thirty years, will just come in and stand right in front of him.

On my first day on the job in London I was involved in an incident. I was photographing some East German movie stars when another photographer came over and hit me twice in the head with his Speed Graphic. Needless to say, I hit him back. This resulted in the photographer's telephoning the editor of the *Daily Sketch* to complain—but afterward, whenever I turned up for a job the other photographers gave me a wide berth.

I was on the *Sketch* in London no more than two years before I moved to the *Daily Express,* around 1958. I was with the *Express* for two years, then went to *Queen Magazine,* a women's fashion monthly. There were a lot of interesting things happening in London at the time. British films, music, books, and fashion were beginning to make an impact on the world; soon everyone would know of the Beatles.

I went back to the *Express* after a year, mainly because I wanted to go to America and the *Express* had an office in New York, assigning reporters and photographers there for two-year stints. I had always wanted to go to America because of the range that American journalism offers.

There are some pictures that are personal milestones; I look back on them and think, "That picture was important" or "This picture resulted in that." The pillow-fight picture of the Beatles was one of these. It was taken in 1964 at the George V Hotel in Paris after Brian Epstein told them "She Loves You" had just been named the number one song in America. It was mainly because of the pillow-fight picture that they asked me to go on tour with them. The *Express* sent me to America with the Beatles, and I never went back to England to live.

I worked for the *Express* while trying to get started in American journalism. All of the American magazines wanted color, and as a news photographer I'd been working only in black and white. There was no call for color in newspapers. I had to learn about color film, about using new techniques, and how to work in a studio with lights. I had to learn to do many new things, but newspapers had already prepared me to get that one picture that would tell the story. My Fleet Street training was extremely important; it taught me to go straight to the center as fast as I could, to get to the guts of the story.

No matter how many newspapers or magazines I was published in, it wasn't until I finally got an assignment from *Life* that I ever thought I might be on my way to becoming a photojournalist. My first assignment for *Life* came in 1968. Although the story never ran, the editors liked my pictures of an artist named R. Crumb. Soon after that, I went on my first big assignment—to Chadron, Nebraska. I did quite a bit of work for *Life*

until, while covering the Paris Peace Talks in 1972, I heard the news that *Life* was folding.

Photojournalism is a very tough field, with a lot of photographers competing for very, very few jobs. Photojournalism is not for the shy and retiring. Anybody who thinks it is soon gets a rude awakening. You have to put your camera in positions that at times can be offensive or an affront to people's privacy. I think that most of the great pictures have been taken under this sort of duress.

Photojournalism brings those private moments to you. It puts those moments on a page, to be looked at over and over again. Photojournalism shows what the television camera misses. It is the essential detail, the essence of a story—of a moment. More than just illustrating a story, the pictures are the main event.

The first photograph I ever had published was of a roe deer, taken in Glasgow's Calder Park Zoo, which my father founded. I was sixteen at the time. I gave the picture to the *Glasgow Evening Times* and waited and waited, until I thought nothing was going to happen. When they used it several months later, I was so proud. (Thornton Pickard plate camera)

Prince Philip, Duke of Edinburgh, had just been made president of Edinburgh University. The ceremony became a riotous affair, with the students showing their appreciation by throwing toilet paper and flour at him. This picture helped me win a British Press Photographer of the Year award in 1957.

When I asked the *Daily Mail* office to develop the film for me (my paper, the *Sketch,* was part of the same newspaper group), I made the mistake of telling them I had a picture of the toilet paper flying through the air, which their photographer had missed. When the plate went into the developer, the printer turned the light on in the darkroom. As a result, this picture is only half the frame; the other half was fogged—deliberately. It was not unusual to sabotage the competition.

One afternoon in 1956 I was walking around the Botanical Gardens in Glasgow looking for picture situations for the newspaper when I happened upon some Glasgow boys up to some mischief. They were cooling off in the fountain, during what was called a "Glasgow heat wave," even though the temperature was no more than about 75 degrees. This picture was part of the portfolio that won an award in that year's British Press Photographer of the Year competition.

American sailors from a submarine carrying Polaris missiles are being greeted by Glasgow housewives in 1961. There had been some controversy over whether the sub should be based in Scotland, because it carried nuclear missiles, but these women welcomed them with open arms.

In 1959 I was doing a story on English nannies. I wanted to show how the British aristocracy left much of the day-to-day rearing of their children to these women. It was a bleak, chilly day on a deserted beach at Frinton when I happened upon the two-year-old marquis of Granby, son of the duke of Rutland, bundled up on the way home after a day at the beach with his nanny.

Stories on the royal family are typical for newspaper photographers in Great Britain. Three days before Prince Andrew's second birthday, in February 1961, he and Princess Anne visited Prince Charles in the hospital. It was the first time Prince Andrew had waved and acknowledged the waiting crowds and photographers. The people were delighted that he was following in the tradition of the royal family and had caught on so quickly.

John and Jackie Kennedy came to London in the summer of 1961, after he became president. London and Paris belonged to Jackie—the press couldn't get enough of her. My assignment for the day was to get her picture. I must have stood outside her sister Lee Radziwill's house for six or seven hours, for it was late in the afternoon when Jackie stepped out to give the waiting photographers a picture.

When the Kennedys left London, I was sent to Paris for their triumphant visit to French President Charles de Gaulle. All day long I chased Kennedy around Paris, never able to get a picture in which I could see his face. The moment came on the Champs Elysées during a ceremony with De Gaulle. I managed to get a height advantage by standing on a wall, and for a brief moment he looked at me. It was raining, and one of his aides tried to hold an umbrella above his head, but he quickly turned it away.

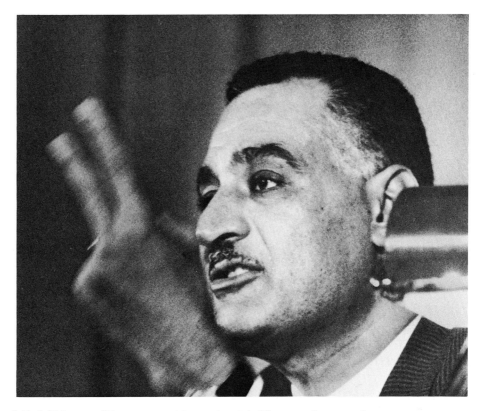

In 1961, President Gamal Abdel Nasser of Egypt was giving a speech to some Egyptian leaders in Cairo. He spoke for five hours nonstop. I couldn't believe a speech would go on for so long. It taught me to always go into an assignment rested, because you never know what to expect.

It was the first assignment with a world leader for the reporter I was with, who usually covered the gossip-nightlife type of story. Indignant at not getting immediate access to Nasser, he asked one of Nasser's aides if he realized how important we were, pompously informing him that after we finished doing the story on Nasser we were going to America to photograph Elvis Presley. I was mortified, but it worked—within half an hour a staff car was driving us out to the palace.

On the day the Berlin wall started to go up in 1961, I got on the first flight out of London to West Berlin. Coincidentally—and coincidence plays a large role in a photojournalist's life—a first-rate Fleet Street reporter named Donald Edgar was on the flight. He spoke perfect German. Getting off the plane, he suggested we try to find the mayor, Willy Brandt. We got to Brandt's office just as he was leaving, but he agreed to go back to his office for an interview and some pictures. He discussed the horrendous situation of Russian troops encircling his city. This photograph makes sense historically because it was taken on the day it mattered, the day the wall went up.

Lord Beaverbrook was proprietor of the *London Daily Express* when I worked there. He was the most important person in my journalistic life. He was Churchill's adviser during World War II, and the minister of aircraft production who got the Spitfire fighter planes ready for the Battle of Britain. Photographing Beaverbrook was to me as much of an honor as photographing Churchill. Beaverbrook was given an eighty-fifth birthday party in 1964 by another Canadian newspaperman, Lord Tompson of Fleet. When Beaverbrook saw me from his seat of honor on the dais at London's Savoy Hotel, he raised his glass in a toast to me.

Later that year, shortly before he died, I was invited to his home at Cherkley. I wanted to do my best on this assignment. I had a very enjoyable day in the sun with Lord and Lady Beaverbrook, listening to stories and being given insights into our profession. Afterward he wrote me a letter calling me a "photographer of the first order." That letter pleased me more than I can say, for to my mind he was without question the greatest journalist I have ever met.

I was pleased at getting an assignment to photograph German Chancellor Konrad Adenauer in 1962. He was eighty-six years old at the time. This was one of the first times I'd been one-on-one with a head of state. I was well aware that Churchill had called him "the greatest of his race since Bismarck."

One of his prides was his garden, so I photographed him in the garden outside his home above the Rhine. Then we went to Bonn, to his office in the Chancellery.

After I photographed him in his office, we said good-bye and he walked back to his desk. While packing up my cameras, I turned around and saw his hand on his head. I moved quickly across the room and took the photograph. He looked up at me, startled, then smiled and said, "More pictures?" I answered, "That was the last one, sir," and left. Many times my last picture of the day has turned out to be the best.

English schoolboy David Field couldn't afford the plane ticket when his class went on a school trip to Norway in 1962. The plane crashed, killing all his classmates. I went to his home outside London to photograph him the morning after. When I got there I found that his parents had sent him fishing to get his mind off the tragedy. I photographed him standing quietly where he liked to fish. He seemed so isolated, fishing all alone.

The pillow fight. It was 3:00 A.M. after a concert in Paris when Brian Epstein told them that "She Loves You" was number one in America, and they knew they would be going there on tour. It was 1964. We were in John Lennon's room in the George V Hotel.

I had thought a pillow-fight picture would be different, but I would never have suggested it if other photographers had been around. It really became quite violent at times, and I think George got the worst of it. This is the one frame that was perfect. There is no way it could have been set up. (wide-angle Rolleiflex, strobe)

John Lennon and his first wife, Cynthia, coming over to America for the first time, in 1964. Brian Epstein, the Beatles' manager, was right behind them. He was never far away. Epstein was extremely helpful to the press—if you were working with the Beatles he never interfered by giving his opinion, and if he did say something it was always positive.

This was my first trip to America, too, and it was a turning point. Even then I knew I would never go back except to visit my family in Scotland. I knew I would stay and work in America. It intrigued me then, and it still does.

When the Beatles stepped off the plane in New York that first time in 1964, they were greeted by shouting newsmen, photographers, and a few fans. I got my cameras ready ahead of time and managed to be the fifth one off the plane. I asked them to turn around and look at me before they stepped down, to give me the picture I wanted of them arriving for the first time.

I think it's a historic picture of the Beatles, but it was never published until a few years ago. It took on a whole new meaning with the passage of time—their first step in America—but at the time I was disap-pointed. I had hoped there would be thousands of screaming fans to meet them. There was a crowd, but nothing in comparison with the crowds that had greeted them elsewhere. Later we learned the fans had been kept away by the police.

I didn't wire the picture to London, because they weren't interested unless there were hysterical fans about. London had in mind a sort of Broadway ticker-tape welcome. Nothing short of that would have been acceptable for the front page of the paper after the way the Beatles had been received in Europe.

RULES OF THE GAME

Certain qualities are essential to a photojournalist. First, you must have an inherent love of photography; next, a strong determination to succeed and a willingness to put everything else second to your work. You also need a sense of history, an awareness of human behavior, physical stamina, a fascination with gossip, a survival instinct, a naive belief in yourself, and a bit of luck.

There are a few things I always say when I'm asked for advice by someone just starting out.

Get a job on a local newspaper is the first thing I always tell a young photographer. Do any kind of event a local newspaper will send you to photograph; get the necessary experience there before going out on your own. To be good at photography you must first take photographs, *lots* of photographs. It can't be done by taking two or three rolls a week. It's very hard to become really good in your spare time, because you're trying to make pictures too artistic, too special. The local paper gives you the chance to take picture after picture, day after day. You can learn technique at photography school, there is a supportive atmosphere in a camera club, but there is nothing like practical on-the-job experience.

Get together a portfolio of your best photographs. The pictures should be what you consider your best work. Include a variety that shows what you can do in different situations, that you know how to use equipment and know lighting. You're better off with ten good pictures than with ten good pictures mixed in with twenty mediocre ones. Your book should not be boring. Don't make all the pictures the same focal length, but vary them with different lenses, some close-up, some middle distance, and even an infinity shot. Don't make your book too depressing. A lot of photographers photograph a lot of sad people and derelicts. Add a pretty girl, something to show movement, something upbeat. Before you show it to an editor, put the book aside, then go back and look at it again. Chances are you'll change some pictures, or at least their sequence. Get some good advice as to what to include, but here again I really think you should go by your own instincts. You're going to get only one chance to show your work to a picture editor or an art director. Give it your best.

If the picture editor wants to talk about photography, be confident but not cocky. Never discuss money as if that were your sole concern. If it is, you're in the wrong business. One well-known picture editor told me the moment money is mentioned, the interview is over. If

and when an assignment comes up, the editor will explain his publication's policy on day and space rates and you'll have everything spelled out for you. Write it down, because each publication is different and you don't want to keep asking each time.

Learn your equipment. Take your camera in hand and get to know it, taking as many pictures as possible until you feel at home with it. You must be able to rely on your equipment without even thinking about it. Handling the camera must become second nature, so that you can concentrate on taking a good picture. When the camera is in good condition and working properly, it feels right. You can feel the film going through the camera and know it is advancing correctly. When I get a new piece of equipment, for instance a new lens, I turn it over and over in my hands, focusing and unfocusing it; or I run an old roll of film through a new camera again and again, testing the autowinder or motor drive until I'm sure everything feels right.

Keep looking at pictures everywhere. In photojournalism content is of the utmost importance, more so than composition. Although you are striving for both, content is the essence. The more you look at pictures, of every kind, the more ideas you get. Study different photographs to see what you like and dislike about them. It will help you learn to quickly frame a picture of your own. Sometimes you see pictures or paintings that are so wonderful they stay in your mind and can be adapted to your needs later. Read and study, but remember that you show a picture editor photographs, not degrees. It's what you can *do* that counts.

Read the newspapers every day. It's simple—reading keeps you in touch with what is going on in the world, and when you read you begin to visualize possible pictures in your mind. If you are going to photograph the secretary of state, it is wise to know a bit about him before you arrive. Do your homework on people, but don't become obsessed by them. Knowing something about them will give you some idea of what to expect when you get there. Keeping up with the news gives you ideas for stories to suggest to picture editors. I suggest about a fourth of the assignments I do, although I never do anything on *spec* (without a firm commitment from a publication, merely hoping to sell the photographs after they are taken). When you suggest ideas to magazines, be sure you can deliver. Young photographers tend to suggest a story with only a vague idea, no research, and not a clue as to how they are going to carry it off.

Create a filing system so your negatives and color slides won't get lost. Stamp every print and slide with your name and copyright notice. Keep a list of what publications have your photographs and when they are returned. Try never to give away negatives; have prints made instead. Make duplicates of your best color slides. (When you're on an assignment, duplicates can't be made until after the publication has made its selection.) Of course, most publications won't want to print from a duplicate, but if the original slide is lost, at least you will have something. Make sure that your slides are returned to you as soon as possible; you don't realize the value of a negative until you lose it. Pictures take on a whole new meaning with the passage of time. Looking back at some old photographs that never saw the light of day, I see they were a lot better than I thought. I see things that editors and I never noticed at the time, when we were looking for a more dramatic effect.

Get a letter stating the terms of the sale in the event that you resell a photograph to a magazine or newspaper other than the assigning publication. It should include the negotiated price, a credit line, and whether or not it is for one-time reproduction use, and it should also state that the negatives must be returned. If you have the details in writing there can be no misunderstanding.

Make your own appointment with a subject, if possible. Don't discuss over the phone what type of pictures you want to take. Just say you won't take long—in other words, that it is not going to be a boring experience. If you say too much the subject may have second thoughts and turn you down. For instance, if you say you want a picture taken in the swimming pool and the congressman has voted to replace a community swimming pool with a high-rise complex, he will begin to think about it and you might get turned down. On the spot, he's more likely to say yes.

Accept that you'll have an erratic family life. Keep your personal problems out of the office. Don't have your wife or husband or friend calling the office to see when you're coming home for dinner. It soon gets around that if they send you out on assignment they'll have to contend with your whole family.

When you're on a two- or three-day story, don't call in to the office too often. Unless you're under pressure because of a closing deadline, you don't have to describe the pictures you've taken blow by blow. In fact, when you explain too much, the picture editor may come back and ask you to try something else that you know is out of the question. It's expected that because you've gone *this* far you can go *that* far. It's better to give the idea either that everything is fine and you have something or that things aren't going as well as you had expected. Never go back wagging your tail that you have some great

photos. Always hold something back. Surprise them. Let them decide when they see the pictures and you'll avoid disappointment.

Don't go by anyone else's instincts. Don't let picture editors, friends, other photographers, teachers, reporters, the subject, his friends, or anyone else set you off in the wrong direction. Listen to the advice of people you respect, but go by your own instincts. Take the pictures *you* see.

Dress for the assignment. I consider this to be very important. In the White House I always wear a suit and tie. During the Nixon Administration two photographers asked me why I always got to the second floor private quarters. I told them that if they stopped dressing like maintenance men their luck might change. We laughed, but I wasn't kidding. Most often I wear a blazer or tweed jacket, either a shirt and tie or a turtleneck sweater, and either gray slacks or blue jeans, depending on whom I'm photographing. Comfortable shoes with soles that won't slip are a must. I don't mimic the dress of the person I'm photographing, but I do try to fit in. From a president to a rock star, dress properly and there is no question you will get further.

In addition to these basics, which have proved useful to me in preparing for an assignment, there are a few essentials that I keep in mind when actually taking photographs and that influence the way I go about my work.

Concentrate totally on what you're doing. That's a big part of it, putting your mind to it. Your attitude will affect the way you take photographs. You come to an assignment with equipment, experience, and attitude. Don't think "I can't do this, I can't do that"—you can do anything. You can amaze yourself. A camera is just a rather expensive tool, and you can do what you want to with it. I feel that if somebody else can do something, then I can, too. From the time an assignment is given to me, I start thinking about it— how to do it, how I want the pictures to look. And during the session I'm totally centered on what I'm doing. Concentration is very important.

Before getting to the assignment, plan what you want to do and have an idea of what the pictures should look like. The majority of people I photograph I've never met before, and I must convey right away that it's not going to be an unpleasant experience. If I've done my homework I'll have an idea of what kind of people they are and how to approach them. You must have a plan of what you want the pictures to look like, even though the plan may change. If you go in with nothing in mind, that's what you'll come out with—nothing.

When I'm with celebrated people, the short time in which to get the pictures is like gold. There's never enough time, so I can't waste it stumbling around for ideas. I have to size things up very quickly and then take control and tell them what I'd like them to do, what I want, watching all the while for the revealing instant that will make the best picture. I can't tell them to sit in the grass when they want to sit in a chair, or they'll look at me like I'm daft. I've got to bring them out slowly, and I always have a plan on how to get them to this place or that. When I have got to the point where I can pop the idea, it's very hard for them to refuse.

Photograph whatever you see as soon as you arrive. I got this advice my first week in Fleet Street, sitting in a pub. A well-known photographer named David Johnston told me that no matter where you go, any assignment at all, photograph everything you see, whatever is around you, as soon as you get there. It sounded elementary at the time, but it has proved to be the soundest advice I've ever been given. The photographer who waits for something to happen is missing what is actually happening. You are there to record, not to become a part of the event. (Invariably almost the opposite holds true in a controlled situation like a fashion sitting, when you must wait for the fantasy to be created before the photography begins.)

If you have a chance to photograph someone and you don't, and later find out that he was the biggest British spy of the century, it can haunt you. I met Kim Philby in Beirut in 1961. He invited several journalists and me out to lunch. Afterward I could have taken a group picture of all of us having a jolly time drinking and laughing, but I didn't. I hope this never happens to me again.

Select the instant to photograph. You must quickly decide what to photograph and what to let pass. Selecting which moment is the telling one is what can separate you from the others.

Try to be the last to leave. Stay as long as you can. The assigning editor must be able to rely upon you not to leave the scene until it's all wrapped up. The last thirty minutes can make all the difference in finding the picture you're looking for.

Don't be overawed by your subject. This is so basic, yet I see it happen all the time. That's why it is almost impossible for a very young or inexperienced photographer to maneuver with a celebrated person. He is overawed by the surroundings, by the people, by the circumstances; in a word, he's intimidated. It doesn't just have to do with age; it's a matter of attitude and experience. I'm not in awe. Not now. A tiny little bit, but it's under control. It comes with experience in photographing people.

You learn to know exactly where you're going. If I have half an hour with the president, I know he would like to sit at the desk reading papers—doing nothing, photographically speaking—but I have to get more. So I say, "Mr. President, I'd like you to do this and that. Let's see what we can do in just thirty minutes." In half an hour I have to get him doing all he would normally do in a day. I can't be afraid to push a little to get what I want. I care about the subject's feelings, but my own feelings are more important. I'm the one who's left looking at the pictures.

Keep your distance from your subject. Although I like or at least respect almost everyone I photograph, there must be a certain distance to ensure objectivity; a road away from too much familiarity; the no-man's-land of privacy that neither of us enters. Even in the closest one-on-one situation you cannot allow yourself to be manipulated by the person you're photographing.

Always be prepared for the unexpected. You must be able to change your moods and your approach the way you would change your clothes or the channel on the television set. Things may not go as smoothly as you thought they would. Your subject may show up with an arm in a sling when you had expected a gymnastic performance. In newspaper photography you can rush from backstage at the ballet to an airplane crash to a reception for royalty, all in one day. These things do happen, so be prepared for the unexpected. The only way you'll get the pictures is by staying alert, prepared to change course without batting an eye.

Keep moving; mobility is essential. Pictures must have some drama in them. You have to be able to move around to get them—ready to move on a moment's notice, not weighted down by too much equipment. Your equipment must be in good repair and you must be in good physical shape to be mobile. The hours are long, the camera bag gets heavy as the day wears on, and you can never tell when you'll be up for forty-eight hours while an important news story is breaking.

Keep working under extreme pressure. To keep photographing in a chaotic situation is the measure of a photojournalist. Focusing totally on what you're competing for—the best picture—you must react like a horse with blinkers on, oblivious to the turmoil around you.

Make every moment count. You will probably have only a short time in which to photograph someone famous. A news event won't repeat itself because you were busy changing the film. The point is to always be looking, and if you see something taking shape, don't let it pass. Don't miss it. Make every moment count. When you're hot, when you're moving with somebody, keep going; keep going to the point of boring him. Keep pushing. If you have somebody like Brooke Shields and she's jumping and doing all kinds of things for you, keep her going as long as you can. Don't say, "That's enough, thank you very much," and leave. Say, "Let's keep going, this is really good." When you have her really posing, really performing, really relaxed, don't stop. Keep making suggestions. You don't know when you'll get the opportunity again.

I am aware of all of these things when I'm taking pictures. Keeping them foremost in my mind helps me get better pictures, and getting better pictures is what the business is all about. No matter how mundane the assignment may be, there is always one good picture to be taken, and possibly a great one.

When I photographed President Jimmy Carter in his office in late 1979, I asked him if he ever looked out the window. He said, "Whenever I've got a moment." I asked him to look out. He did, even though he appeared tired and worried about the U.S. hostages in Iran. With the glass between us like a wall, it's as if I'm not even there. I think a window between people really isolates them. To me, the picture shows the loneliness of the Oval Office. (24 mm)

Nancy Reagan had been campaigning with her husband in New Hampshire in 1976. She turned and caught her husband's eye and smiled as he helped her on with her coat. It was a private moment in a public gathering. (50 mm)

Even in the midst of Watergate in the spring of 1974, Pat Nixon carried on. She found time to speak to a delegation of Republican women from Virginia in the second floor Blue Room as if nothing out of the ordinary were going on. (24 mm)

Overleaf: Placing someone in a different or unexpected situation can make the picture more interesting. Betty Ford was photographed for *Vogue* magazine before she moved into the White House in 1974, while her husband was vice-president. I found a vacant field near their home in Virginia and, knowing she had wanted to be a model when she was younger, asked her to lie down in the grass to show off her dress. It was an opportunity for her to be a model, and I think she handled it well. (85 mm)

Prowling the streets at night in a car, I was looking for pictures during the August 1965 riots in the Watts section of Los Angeles. With police sirens wailing and buildings smoldering around me, I came across these scenes in the early hours of the morning. (28 mm, strobe)

Getting the relevant picture to illustrate breaking news is what newspaper photography is all about. You have to have a love for news and journalism and drama and crisis. There is nothing I like better than the challenge of a good news story.

One challenge came when the Boston Strangler, Albert de Salvo, escaped from an institution for the criminally insane near Boston in 1966. I flew to Boston, rented a car, turned on the car radio, and headed toward the asylum. Hearing a newsflash, I discovered I was headed in the wrong direction. I turned around, and arrived on the main street of the town of Lynn just at the precise moment that he was apprehended in a shoe store, huddled in a corner, dressed as a sailor. In the photograph de Salvo (*center*) is being led down the stairs of the Lynn police station by the detective who caught him. (wide-angle Rolleiflex)

Brooke Shields was thirteen when this picture was taken late in 1978 for the year-end issue of *People*. She came to the studio with her mother, Teri. The idea I had was to dress Brooke as a very young ballerina, with model Kay Zunker as a harlequin dancing behind her. She posed as a ballerina, but Teri whispered to me that Brooke liked the harlequin outfit, which designer Barbara de Portago had made especially for the sitting. She changed into it and really came alive, jumping and having a good time, to the point where the seamless paper got rumpled and torn, but we kept going anyway. Although I have photographed her since, this is my favorite picture. (wide-angle Rolleiflex)

Francis Ford Coppola was directing Diane Keaton and Al Pacino in a scene from *The Godfather* outside Radio City Music Hall in 1971. It was cold outside and late at night, and the sidewalk had been blocked off for the filming. Diane Keaton was doing her face-relaxing exercises before the scene began, to limber up, much as an athlete would warm up before a game. (50 mm)

Eighty-eight-year-old Pierre Monteux, one of the greatest symphony conductors in the world, was simply crazy about fire engines. In London in 1963 to conduct the London Symphony Orchestra, he went to Fire Brigade Headquarters and lined up with his temporary colleagues for a demonstration in his honor. He donned a special fireman's hat and stood among the firemen, shouting "Bravo" as the firemen scaled their ladders and dangled from windows for him. (28 mm)

Twelve years later, in 1975, the situation presented itself again when Mayor Abe Beame, the five-foot-two-inch mayor of New York, attended a ceremony to honor city firemen for heroism. At the time Beame was making budget cutbacks that would cause many firemen to be laid off, but he lined up in the midst of the firemen to watch the ceremony, and the earlier picture was accidentally re-created. (wide-angle Rolleiflex)

When I flew to Nashville to photograph Dolly Parton for *People* magazine, her manager told me that because of her busy schedule I could have only one and a half hours with her at her home. In this situation I had to push as far as I could to get the pictures I wanted. Dolly is very professional and pleasant to work with. She changed outfits for me; let me photograph her playing in her walk-in closet, combing one of her wigs, lounging on her bed in a robe; and then she sang for me while playing the guitar, piano, and banjo.

The photographs were going well and my time was up. It was pouring rain outside, and I suggested that she go out on her second-floor balcony and wave good-bye to me. She did, and I was on my way back to the office with enough situations to make a picture story. (28 mm, strobe)

Being prepared for the unexpected and taking advantage of it are a part of being mobile. I was on assignment, canoeing down the Snake River in Idaho with Bobby Kennedy, his family, and their friends in the summer of 1966. Bobby had pushed one of his daughters into the water earlier in the day. She waited for the right moment to get even, and in he went. (500 mm)

I had read somewhere that Jules Feiffer imagined himself as Fred Astaire dancing through life and had used this fantasy in some of his cartoons. My idea was to ask him to re-create this fantasy while I photographed him. When he arrived at the studio in 1976, I asked him to draw a life-size self-portrait. He worked very quickly on the seamless white paper background that I put up, and drew the picture in no more than ten minutes. Having an idea of what I wanted ahead of time helped me get a more interesting picture. (wide-angle Rolleiflex)

Frank Sinatra gave a benefit performance for the University of Santa Clara in 1974. After a two-year retirement, he was tense as he waited for his cue to go on. Once he stepped before the footlights, the smile appeared, the crowd rose to its feet, and the relaxed Sinatra you'd expect took over.

I maneuvered around the stage to get an overall picture of the crowd reacting to his performance. (24 mm)

Janis Joplin jumped onto the stage unexpectedly, wearing a funny hat, and started bouncing around while Tina Turner was singing during a Rolling Stones concert at Madison Square Garden in 1968. I didn't know who she was at first. I actually thought for a moment it was Mick Jagger in drag, and quickly took a few frames. It was early in the concert, but I moved through the crowd to the front and started to work because the crowd was screaming and shouting, so I thought there might be something there. Then someone told me who she was. I wish I had worked harder to get better pictures. The biggest event might not always be the most obvious. That's why it's a good idea to start photographing as soon as you arrive on a story. (85 mm)

THE ASSIGNMENT

Planning for an assignment depends, naturally, on what kind of story it is: feature, hard news, or fashion. A feature story is one that is suggested by editors, writers, or photographers and can be angled any number of different ways. A feature story is planned in advance, there is more time to get pictures, and the photographer can orchestrate the situation. A hard news story takes care of itself. It's a story that goes its own way and doesn't do what you tell it to. A hard news story can't be repeated; you must capture what is happening at the moment. Fashion is, well, fashion. It's a fantasy to get people to buy what you're selling.

The most exciting part of an assignment for me is when the telephone rings and I'm actually given the job; then my imagination goes to work. Pictures flash in my head—what can go wrong, what can go right. I find the challenge and expectation exhilarating. Delivering the pictures is the hard part.

Many decisions are made before an assignment ever begins. Usually the picture editor will explain why you are getting the assignment and how he sees the story. A good picture editor won't impose his views on you, but will tactfully let you know what is important and what the editors feel is relevant to their magazine or newspaper. A good photographer will keep within the bounds of what is wanted—if they want a funny picture, I'll think up a funny picture. The picture editor can tell me what they're looking for, giving directions and boundaries, but then it's up to me. My imagination and creativity must come into it, but I don't want to waste all afternoon photographing someone with his wife and dog and get back to the office to hear that they didn't want the wife or the dog in the pictures.

The picture editor gives the assignment and, along with the editor, looks at the pictures when they come in and edits them. The pictures are then given to the art director, who lays out the story.

Having gotten the assignment, I immediately start thinking about the pictures I want to take and making up a plan. Is one picture wanted or a whole picture story? Can I speak to the subject to move the story along; orchestrate it; or will circumstances take it completely out of my control?

When I get an assignment, I always ask if it's black and white or color or both. Sometimes the picture editor just doesn't know, because of the closing deadlines on the story. (Color pages must go to press sooner, so if the text hasn't been written in time, your color pictures could be converted to black and white, which will affect the quality slightly.) For this reason, I try to take both black and white and color on most assignments. It's easier to take black and white on the run, going from daylight to fluorescent light to hardly any light at all; I don't worry too much about exposure, because it can be corrected in the darkroom. With color you have a different set of problems and you have to think more about lighting. I don't think that only pretty things should be in color and only stark things in black and white. To me, the unexpected use of color adds impact, an added dimension to a stark subject.

There are many decisions to be made before an assignment begins. If the assignment is on location, will I need a flash or a strobe, or will natural light suffice? What effect do I want to achieve? It depends on the nature of the assignment, the location and the time of day.

When I've gone wrong in preparing for an assignment, it's usually at the beginning, by taking either too much or too little equipment. For example, I once had to photograph Julie Eisenhower for the cover of *Good Housekeeping*. I didn't want to disturb her by bringing strobes into the private quarters of the White House. The day turned out to be dull and overcast, and that's just what my pictures were like. It was very disappointing. So it's not *always* best to be mobile.

When I take my strobes, which are heavy and bulky, I also take an assistant. I brief my assistant on what I'm thinking, though I don't want his opinions unless I ask for them. All I want is for him to put up the lights where I want them and get things ready. I certainly don't want an assistant who's going to hustle business for himself or who might bring along a camera and take pictures over my shoulder when I'm not looking. And this does happen.

In the studio I always use an assistant; on location I usually don't. The assistant comes to the studio at least an hour before everyone else arrives, to get everything ready. He arranges the cameras and lenses and the film I want and puts the lights up. He also puts up the seamless paper background used for most studio photography. The color of the paper is a matter of taste, but I prefer light or medium gray, with dark gray and white as my next choices. In retrospect, I think my studio pictures that hold up best are the ones with these neutral backgrounds, rather than those with brighter ones. In a studio picture I see the subject better when the background is incidental.

If it is to be a cover session, there will usually be a hairdresser and makeup person, and possibly a stylist, who brings and organizes the clothes and accessories if we are using designer clothes rather than the subject's own wardrobe. When the photography begins I don't want a lot of faces staring at the subject, or at me for that matter, and I clear the studio except for my assistant. I call in one of the others from time to time when I think the hair or makeup might need touching up, but otherwise I prefer to work one-on-one. If it is a fashion session, the editor will sit at the back and confer with me from time to time, but her assistants and crew stay in the dressing room unless we need them.

When I was photographing Farrah Fawcett for the cover of *People,* I asked everyone to leave the room and wait in the other part of the studio. When they left, she said, "I'm glad you did that. I hate people looking at me all the time." I agreed with her. If I feel the presence of someone trying to be protective by giving opinions, it's very disconcerting and makes me angry. I know that every time I've made mistakes in a studio, it's been because I lost my concentration. I feel awkward with others around. If I'm going to get embarrassed taking pictures, then the pictures are going to be bad.

I have learned never to take anyone for granted, especially if we haven't met before. Regardless of what I've heard about how congenial someone is, not until I am comfortable and have built up some confidence do I relax into the situation. I talk all the time, to the subject, but mostly to myself, to get him relaxed and to get me going—for if I can get myself going, I can get him going. My emotional state as well as that of the subject affects the photographs. I always photograph in a state of nervous tension, even though my mood and approach must change with each assignment. I don't like to come in on the same level again and again. If I'm on a story for several days, and come back for a second or third take, I like to come in on another level with new ideas, fresh ideas; to photograph in a completely different way that may add a new dimension to the story.

Sometimes I can get so close to people that I'm just not catching the story, or I can get really bored with a story and wish I were photographing something else. Then sometimes the picture editor will come up with some good ideas that help me see what can be done.

I'm hesitant to confide in picture editors completely during an assignment, because their response can be very negative: "I don't like these ideas" or "That doesn't sound very interesting"—yet when the pictures come in and are good, they like them. Meanwhile, I wasted all that time and energy thinking of other ideas and trying to get other pictures that weren't necessary, when I should have been working to perfect my first idea. What I like to bring back to the editors is a pleasant surprise.

When I work on a story and I'm putting my heart into it, I'm very secure, but the minute my pictures are handed in terrible doubts arise. Handing in the film can be like handing in part of my life, and then comes the terrible wait while it's being processed. So many things go through my head: Should I have used a different lens? Was the exposure right? I'm always sure I had the wrong lens in. Or what if the key picture, which is the opening picture in my mind, doesn't work out; do I have another to compensate?

I think of things I might have done. I'm uncertain, depressed, insecure, knowing my work is going to be judged. Waiting to hear if the picture editor and the managing editor both like the pictures is excruciating. There is such a fine line between success and failure that I want to know their reaction right away, that subjective opinion that can make or kill a picture. Yet when I'm working, it's just the opposite and I'm quite confident of doing my best. I feel less insecure on a routine assignment when I know I've done a competent job than on a big assignment where everything hinges on my producing some good pictures.

I don't worry about the editors selecting the wrong pictures. They know their job. They want the best pictures, and if they don't choose them that's too bad; there's nothing I can do about it. I'm not always good, and when I'm not, good editing can get me off the hook. Editing can help make the best of a mediocre job. Sometimes good pictures can be rejected simply for lack of space in the magazine.

If the response to the pictures is negative, I try to learn from my mistakes and not forget the next time. If my pictures are really bad, I can't wait to forget about them—if the pictures are lousy, then everything is lousy. My idea is not to go out expecting a great time. The great time is no good if the pictures aren't. If things go badly, learn from it. You can't do anything about it except start over again, fresh. Those photographers who can't take criticism and rejection and keep going won't stay in the business long, however sensitive their work may be.

After an assignment is over, I like to go on to the next one. By the time the pictures are published I'm usually engrossed in a new story. Yet, I'm always excited when my pictures appear in print. When I see the final layouts of my work I like to sit and look at them—usually thinking about how I could have made them better. From pictures that are really exceptional to those that don't make much of an impact on me, I always try to learn something from each assignment that can be applied to the next.

I asked several editors what they look for in both a photographer and a photograph, curious myself as to what their answers would be.

John Loengard, *Life,* picture editor:

I don't look at photographers. Their appearance and character don't mean much. I do care about their enthusiasm at the thought of doing something for *Life,* but frankly, I can't think of when I've met anything but an overabundance of enthusiasm, because good outlets are scarce in photography.

I want to see something peculiar and meaningful in a photograph. I don't care if it is correct or proper. Is it interesting? Is it important? Is it moving? Is it new? Is it good to look at?

Mel Scott, *Life,* assistant picture editor:

In a photographer, the most important aspect is industriousness; a sense of creativity; a willingness to work hard; a sense of developing a story; and an ability to take photographs that are out of the ordinary.

In a photograph, I look for content; pictures with an unusual twist; and photographs that are fun to look at.

Karen Mullarkey, *New York* Magazine, picture editor:

The best photographers are the ones who don't tell you how difficult, trying, exhausting it was to get the picture; they just get it ... every time. When I make an assignment I work from my intuition and instincts— would the subject like this photographer or that one? Would it be better to be smooth, or would ruffled feathers produce the special electricity that I am always trying to find, create, and inspire? I realize that certain photographers possess greater degrees of technical expertise, and I certainly consider that every time I have to make an assignment, but technical expertise by itself isn't a guarantee of creative excellence.

I guess that I am continually looking for photographs that I can dream about. I know I have had a successful session if the person's face keeps coming to me in my dreams. Many times I will edit work but not make a final decision until the next day and wait and see which photograph I dream about ... it seems to work for me.

Jordan Schaps, *New York* Magazine, cover editor:

Talent and technique are givens. Then I look for the photographer's ability to understand my concept of what the specific job is, and his ability to realize that concept *his* way, carrying it way beyond what I have started him off with. I look for a photographer who will get excited about an assignment and never, never treat work as "just another job." Lastly, I look for his ability to commit himself to taking the best damned picture

imaginable, and not stopping, settling, or giving in until that is reached. That's my idea of a photographer.

Immediate impact. If I have to figure a photograph out, I probably won't like it. I love photographs that have subtlety and nuance, but only in support of a strong central statement. I am moved by and respond to the "broad stroke."

Mary Dunn, *People,* picture editor:

Sensitivity, imagination, doggedness, and guile. Particularly in shooting human beings. I once read that there was a group of primitives somewhere in the world who refused to be photographed because they were afraid the camera would steal their souls. I sometimes think modern society feels pretty much the same way. Faced with a camera, most people lock away their souls, become wooden and false. Photographing human beings is largely a matter of breaking down barriers—one after another—to catch a glimpse of the real person behind them.

The *basic* qualifications a photographer must have are: *talent:* he must have an eye—the ability to see a photograph when it exists in front of him; *creativity*— the ability to make a picture when one doesn't exist in front of him; and, *extensive technical knowledge* to ensure that no good but difficult picture will ever be forfeited.

If, on top of all of the requirements I've mentioned, a given photographer has flair and, very important, a sense of humor, he's got a real future at *People.*

A good photograph for *People*—or any other publication—should stop the viewer as he flips the pages and make him want to read the story. A good picture should move or amuse, intrigue or outrage you—it must touch you somehow, and it should tell you something you didn't know. The best pictures do so profoundly. Like poetry, they capture the essence of a person, distill a moment or an emotion, concentrating it for power and greater impact.

Mary Carroll Marden, *People,* assistant picture editor:

When I assign a photographer, my hope is that the result of the take will be a memorable photograph— not just an adequate one. The person who will get this picture is the real professional—the person who *wants* to take that memorable picture and *works* at getting it. The photographer I'm looking for is the one who wants to shoot the story better than anyone else, who is sensitive and bright enough to know how to get the picture and hungry enough to get it no matter what. There are, of course, many other things that come to mind in making an assignment. Naturally I want the magazine well represented, I want to have a lively exchange about what to shoot before the photographer goes out, and I want deadlines respected. I want enthusiasm.

I, of course, love to find the photograph that jumps out at me from a contact sheet. I know immediately that it will work. But the photograph that catches a special moment, captures a mood, one that makes me laugh, and finally one that lets me know a little more about the person, is an image that pleases me. That's what I look for in a photograph.

Robert N. Essman, *People,* art director:

As the art director of a magazine about human beings, my only concern is that the pictures, sharp and well composed, tell an honest, possibly witty, perhaps humorous or poignant story about the person.

David Breul, East/West Network, editor:

A photographer should be quick, flexible, and skillful enough to use more than one approach in covering an assignment, leaving it up to the editor and art director ultimately to choose the best point of view. Beyond these basics, however, what can be even better is a photographer whose own charm, wit, and style enable him or her to enter—and, in a certain sense, control—a situation or environment that may be closed off to others.

In a photograph I look for an unexpected expression or emotion, an unusual relationship or sense of movement, that suggests an interesting twist to the personality or scene.

Sexy Movies? Chadron, Neb. Tries Gentle Persuasion

by HUGH MOFFETT

The Chadron, Nebraska, story appeared in the May 30, 1969, issue of *Life* about a band of women in a small town who were up-in-arms about the x-rated movies being shown in the local cinema. A week earlier the theater owner had presented *Rumplestilt-skin* and the audience turnout was less than enthusiastic, but with *Isobel and Teresa,* an x-rated French film, there was standing room only. This was my first big assignment for *Life.* Unfortunately the negatives were lost in 1972, when the magazine closed.

Mary Tyler Moore had come to the studio for a photo session for a *People* cover story when the movie *Ordinary People* was released in 1980. Afterward she changed clothes and asked me to take a picture for her to send to her fans. This was one of the few times I have done personal photography for a star. Mary Tyler Moore said she was pleased, but usually it's hard to please people because they have very definite ideas as to how they should look. It's much harder to please an individual than a magazine. Magazines are interested in good pictures—not in their "good side." (Hasselblad, 80 mm)

Waiting in a TV studio to photograph Suzanne Somers and her *Three's Company* co-stars for the cover of *People* in 1977, I was told there wasn't much time. The only place I could put up seamless paper for the background was on the edge of their set between the coffee machine and the men's room. It was the busiest thoroughfare in Burbank. Everytime someone went to the toilet, the wind from the door blew the seamless paper down.

When the three stars were ready I gave orders that no one was to use the toilet while I was photographing the cover. They stayed about five minutes before being called back to their set. In that time I took five or six rolls and proceeded from a straightforward pose to the antics of John Ritter biting Suzanne Somers's shoulder. (85 mm)

On the Beatles' first trip to Paris in 1964, just before their trip to America, we stayed at the George V Hotel. In the lobby was a bust of Napoleon. As we passed it every day, we remarked on how much it looked like John Lennon. I had the idea of having John pose in front of the statue, not only because they looked alike but because they had the same kind of haircut. The picture was never used. An annoying fact about newspaper photography is that while there can be several good pictures from a day's take, one picture is chosen and the rest are filed. (wide-angle Rolleiflex, strobe)

Farrah Fawcett had been in my studio all afternoon for a cover for *People* magazine in 1981. The black-and-white photographs for the inside feature were to be done the next day. I always keep in mind that with someone as busy as she is, the schedule might change at the last minute, so I decided to do some black and white while she was there. I asked her to sit on my living-room couch for a quick photograph, then I went downstairs with her as she left, photographing her in the telephone booth outside my apartment. (I was really popular with my doormen after that.) It was raining and beginning to get dark, which gave the photo an effect I liked. The next day her publicist called to say Farrah had a sore throat, so *People* used the two situations I'd taken, and the story closed on time. (50 mm)

Natassia Kinski was sitting on the bank of the Seine on a very wet autumn day when this picture was taken. Timing played a large part in its not being published. It was taken for *People* in 1979, before the movie *Tess* had been released in America, and she was unrecognizable here. The story was postponed. After the movie opened and was nominated for an Academy Award, *People* decided to revive the story on her. She had cut her hair for a new movie role, so new pictures had to be taken. (24 mm)

Author John Cheever sits drinking coffee in the kitchen of his restored Dutch house in Ossining, New York. His daughter's golden retriever basks in the doorway. Cheever is shy but very well mannered. The photograph is an outtake from one of my earliest assignments for *Life,* in 1969. (35 mm)

It's hard not to take a funny picture of Gilda Radner. When I photographed her in 1977 she told me that as a kid she wanted to dance like Rita Hayworth and that she had wished for Rita's face. I told her to hold the painting in front of her face and dance like Rita. It dawned on me afterward that maybe she should have been dancing with her own portrait covering her face. (28 mm, strobe)

 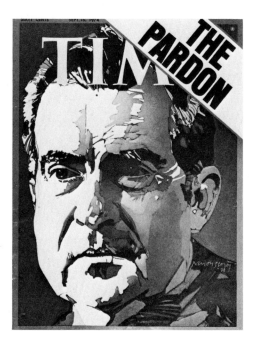

The black-and-white portrait of President Nixon is a color conversion that was used as a *Life* cover in 1973. A print was filed in the *Life* picture collection, where copies of everything used in the magazine are kept. Several months later I picked up *Time* magazine and was surprised to see a painting exactly like my picture on the cover. When I asked, *Time* told me they had given the photograph to an artist to copy. They had neglected to ask my permission or even tell me they were going to use the picture in that way. Credit was given only to the artist in the magazine. (50 mm, tungsten film)

President Ford, painted especially for Vogue by Andy Warhol.

American *Vogue* did basically the same thing. They asked me for a file photograph of Gerald Ford, who had just become president. When I asked what issue the picture would appear in, they told me April. I opened the April 1975 issue to find Andy Warhol had painted my picture. I was surprised and disappointed not to have been told about this in advance.

These incidents pose a problem for a photographer. Both magazines should have had the courtesy to ask before they took the liberty of having an artist paint my work. It's a good idea to find out how editors intend to use your photographs. (28 mm)

After his autobiographical film *All That Jazz* was released in 1979, I was assigned to photograph Bob Fosse for *People*. He doesn't like to be photographed, and it took several calls back and forth to finally pin him down. When I got to his apartment he was fine. We took Polaroid pictures of each other and inscribed them "To my best friend," and generally had a good time together. He struck the classic Fosse pose, which was what I wanted to get before I left.

It was an ordinary take, and the managing editor of *People,* Richard Stolley, thought it was more effective to airbrush out the whole background. I was worried about the effect, but I must admit it was interesting. I think it is generally accepted that an art director or editor may manipulate a picture to make it more interesting. After all, the editor has the final say. (Hasselblad, 50 mm, bounced strobe)

President Nixon giving a televised farewell to his staff on his last day as president, in August 1974. I wanted to be very mobile to get the picture I had in mind. I went with only two cameras, three extra lenses, and no tripod, so I could move around for the angle I wanted. I knew they would all be upset, and I wanted to get Pat looking at him as he spoke.

Richard Stolley, managing editor of *People,* wanted to come in close on President and Mrs. Nixon. The picture was cropped when it was published in *People,* which I thought made it more dramatic. It later won an award in the University of Missouri Pictures of the Year competition.

When you're working very quickly on a news story, the luxury of framing must take second place to your main purpose, getting the gist of what is happening. (200 mm)

EQUIPMENT

I come to an assignment with ability and equipment. I must have the right equipment at the right time for the job I'm doing. The equipment I use must be dependable. I don't want to have to think about the equipment when I'm working; I want to concentrate on the pictures.

My favorite camera is the one I'm using at the time I happen to take a good picture. The feel of a camera in my hand is very important to me; it has to fit right. People who know what they're doing hold a camera assertively, with authority. You have to hold it aggressively, not roughly but firmly, with confidence. That way, you'll take better pictures.

Lightness is another essential factor, along with sturdiness. I use the Minolta system for 35 mm and have for years—they're lightweight, yet strong. The Minolta lenses are very fast and incredibly sharp. I use the Minolta XK body series with motor drive, but I prefer the XD11 or XGM with autowinder for mobility when I'm on location. When I'm working on location I prefer to use autowinders not motor drives because they are lighter, and yet allow you to bracket without taking your eyes off the subject.

When planning for an assignment I choose my equipment slowly and methodically, keeping in mind what the assignment is. Is it one day in town, two weeks on location, a feature or hard news story? These things affect what and how much equipment I take. In deciding what to take, I think of a similar assignment. I think about my priorities, what I want to accomplish on the story. I try to match the equipment to the assignment. While packing, I keep reminding myself of what went wrong on a similar job. By going wrong I mean not having something I needed at the time. Naturally, I have to cover myself in case something breaks, but I don't like to travel with too many cameras. Lightness is very important to me and mobility is absolutely essential. I can move much more easily if I'm not weighted down. If I've worked all day and am tired and don't think I have any pictures yet, the last half hour is vital. I can't be weighted down.

When offered a big assignment like going to Africa for *Life*, I keep thinking about what equipment I will need. I must take everything I need to a place like Africa. The word here is *need*, because I find it equally as bad to take too much as it is to take too little. Too much and you're not mobile; too little and you're strapped.

I carry as much equipment onto the plane as I can so if my luggage gets lost, and it does, I can still work. I keep it with me at all times. This includes some unexposed film, which I take out of the cartons to save space and put in X-ray-proof bags. The rest of the equipment and film goes into the checked luggage and I hope it's going to make it with me. I use nondescript luggage because the heavy silver equipment cases just advertise that you are a photographer and your equipment is more likely to be stolen. When I check luggage with equipment in it, I don't use any labels saying CAMERA EQUIPMENT or FRAGILE. That is just asking to have it stolen.

A tripod is one of the first things I pack. I find a good tripod nearly as important as a good camera. There are certain pictures that just can't be taken without one. Even when I started out I knew I should carry one, but I didn't because they are a bit cumbersome and reduce your mobility. Still, they are useful in so many situations that I have changed my mind. For example, at Riker's Island Prison the light was bad and I had no strobes. I put the camera on a tripod for a long exposure with Ektachrome film and got a prisoner in his cell for the cover of *New York* Magazine. I couldn't have taken that picture without a tripod.

I prefer to pack a very large, strong canvas shoulder bag, the bag used by fishermen, to carry on the plane. I can cram everything into it, including a sweater in case I get cold. The harder, leather bags are heavier, don't give, and won't hold as much, although they provide better protection for the equipment. Though it's not the ideal, I'd rather have the equipment on the plane with me, all bundled up in chamois dustcloths, with the possibility of its being chipped and knocked about a bit, than packed in shipping cartons in a plane going in the opposite direction.

In the large canvas bag I take:

1. Four 35-mm single-lens reflex camera bodies, usually the XD11 or the XGM, with autowinder.

2. Two light meters for flash and natural light.

3. A full range of lenses: the 17 mm; wide angles 20 mm, 24 mm, and 28 mm; the 35 mm; a medium-range 50 mm, 85 mm, 105 mm, 200 mm, and 300 mm, with teleconverters for the 200-mm and 300-mm lenses that double their focal range. I pack more lenses than I'll use each day.

4. A small flash. Whether or not I take a large strobe

unit depends on what I'm doing, but I always go with a small flash. It's simple—if I have no light, I can't take pictures.

5. Extra batteries for cameras and flash. No matter where I go I take extra batteries, for equipment just stops when the batteries run down.

6. Four sync cords for the flash.

7. Gaffer's tape, the thick gray tape that can be torn easily. I use it for everything.

8. X-ray-proof lead bags for exposed film.

9. Pen and paper to mark the film with special developing instructions as I work.

10. A small screwdriver set with changeable head sizes to tighten lenses that become loose.

11. A silk pocket handkerchief to clean the lenses. Years ago, an older photographer told me never to use any cleaning solution on a lens. I doubt it is still good advice today, but I can't get out of the habit of simply using a silk scarf and the steam from my breath to clean a lens.

12. Several filters.

13. Chamois dustcloths to wrap and protect the equipment.

14. A small portable tripod.

15. Film.

In the small canvas bag I take on location each day, I pack:

1. Two 35-mm camera bodies with autowinders.

2. One light meter.

3. Five lenses—usually a 20 mm or 24 mm, a 35 mm, a 50 mm, an 85 mm or 105 mm, and a 200 mm, wrapped in dustcloths.

4. Film, filters, tape, X-ray bags, pen, paper, screwdriver, and silk pocket handkerchief.

5. Tripod.

The rest of the equipment is left in the hotel room until I need it.

The type of film I take depends on the assignment. For black and white I always use Tri-X, 35 mm, 36 exposures. I've been told that Plus-X is a good film, and I tried it a couple of times in the studio but was never satisfied with it. Plus-X is too contrasty for me personally. Tri-X is fast film with an ASA of 400, and even in bad light I know I will get a picture.

For practically everything in color I use Kodachrome 64, 35 mm, 36 exposures. I do not use color negative film. I think Kodachrome 64 is the best all-around color film I've ever used, and I'll use it until something better comes out. It is a slow film with an ASA of 64, but the quality is incredibly sharp. It can't be processed quickly, though. If there is a closing deadline and no time to wait, I will use Ektachrome 64, which can be processed in a couple of hours.

I use Ektachrome 400 for indoor daylight conditions. I try not to use it in bright daylight unless the closing time on the story demands it. I use a warming filter to counteract the blueness of the film. Believe me, suntanned faces are much more acceptable than blue ones.

The pictures I admire most are more straightforward, but I do use filters for certain effects. I occasionally use a polarizer filter with color. It makes the sky dark and everything quite contrasty, and landscapes can almost look like another planet, but I know I can get a certain effect with it even though the picture doesn't necessarily look real.

With Ektachrome I usually ask for a clip test. This involves clipping off a bit of the negative and developing it to see if special processing is called for. It destroys one frame, but it's good insurance—better than ruining a whole roll.

Black and white can be inspected as it's developed. Umpteen times I've been saved without knowing it by a good darkroom technician.

There are times when I use strobe equipment on location—for features, fashion, or a cover story, but never for hard news. In order to get a good "fill" light you must have a good strobe. When I take a strobe unit, I take one 1200-watt box, two heads with stands, umbrellas and reflectors, grounding plugs, extension cords, and current converters for foreign countries, unless I'm using a unit that has the converter built in. In situations where I need less light, I use a 600-watt monoblock. It is lighter-weight and recharges faster than the larger 1200. When I'm using strobes on a feature or in a studio situation, I test exposures by taking a Polaroid. It gives me some idea of what the lighting will be like.

If you don't have your own lights and you have to rent them, know how to use them well before you leave for an assignment. Practice putting them up and taking them down yourself. You can waste so much time with them that the subject gets bored. Putting up the lights is the part that has to go quickly. That is why in the studio or on location I like to use an assistant to set up the lights and make sure they are in sync, and also keep the cameras loaded and the film organized.

When I went to the Caspian Sea to photograph the shah of Iran and his family just before he was overthrown, I carried the heavy strobe all the way. The only picture I used it on was the photograph of the shah sitting with his dog under a picture of some peace doves. I put one light about twenty-four feet across the room from the shah, and I stood about six feet from him for the picture. I used only one light, straight on him. In this case I feel carrying the strobe all that way was worth it.

Knowing I have the best equipment I can have is important in giving me confidence. I want to feel comfortable with my equipment, then forget it, knowing it won't let me down. It must be second nature to me. I must be able to trust my equipment so I can concentrate on taking good pictures.

Mrs. Jimmy Carter with Amy in the private quarters of the White House. I used one floodlight bounced off the ceiling just to give me a fill. The Carters hadn't been giving any photographers access to them, but it was late in 1979, getting nearer to the election, and they wanted some good publicity in a magazine that reached a large audience, like *People*. I asked at the right time and she agreed. (28 mm)

Barbara Walters is an extremely busy woman who doesn't have time to be photographed, but she is relaxed here, sitting on her bed with her daughter, Jacqueline, in 1976. I used one quartz light instead of a strobe to give the effect of natural lighting. (28 mm)

I photographed actor Mark Hamill and his wife and son in Central Park in 1981. Sometimes, to give the impression that something is not set up or posed, it is good to use a telephoto lens. It gives the impression that you're not part of the action. (250 mm)

Rock singer Pat Benatar was rehearsing in a Los Angeles sound stage for a concert tour in 1981. She's got a very powerful voice, even when she's curled up in a little ball. I thought it was interesting that such a huge voice could come from this tiny little body. The photograph was taken with a wide-angle lens and shows an effective way to use the lens without distorting the main figure. (28 mm)

While photographing Suni Agnelli, heir to the Italian Fiat car fortune, in her New York apartment in 1975, I was struck by the lifelike statue of a boy on the floor. I looked twice to make sure he wasn't real; it was so incredibly lifelike I couldn't help but stare at it. I used a tripod with two quartz lights bounced off the wall. I thought detail was important in this picture. (Hasselblad, 50 mm)

I was in Pittsburgh in 1971 when four thousand eighteen-year-olds registered to vote in one day. For this picture of three young men taking the oath I changed from a wide-angle to an 85-mm lens quickly, without looking at the exposure setting. The 85-mm brought the subjects up closer and was the lens I needed. On the contact sheet the frame was so light that I missed the picture when first editing. It was obviously two stops under, but with Tri-X film still very printable, and was the picture used in *Life*.

Sir Winston Churchill went back to his old school, Harrow, each year at Christmastime. This was his last visit, in 1965, before he died. He was being cheered by the boys, who sang out, "And Churchill's name will win acclaim through each new generation." My flash broke, and I had to work off the flash of the photographer next to me to take this picture. You can do this by setting your camera at "B," waiting for the other flash, and then releasing the shutter. (wide-angle Rolleiflex)

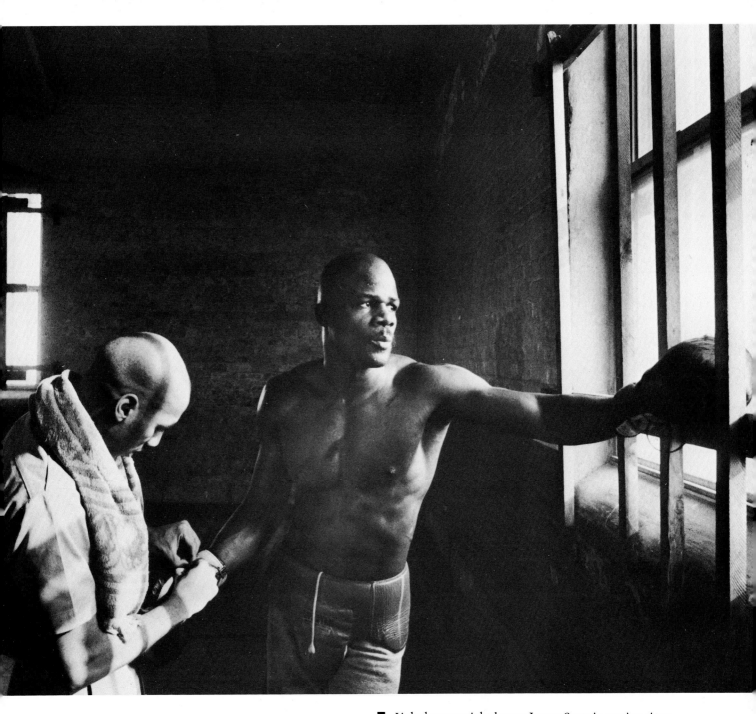

Light-heavyweight boxer James Scott is serving time in Rahway State Prison in New Jersey, where I photographed him for *People* in 1978. He is a polite, clever person and an extremely good boxer. He works out in the prison gym and fights from the prison. He was getting ready for a sparring bout in the prison gym and his hands were being wrapped by fellow inmate Keith Hill. I liked the way the sunlight came through the prison bars. I used only the light from the window and a tripod to get the effect I wanted. (28 mm, tripod)

MOBILITY

Mobility is a key factor, certainly a priority, in not missing an important picture. It involves being able to get to the center of things and start taking pictures immediately; being flexible enough to change your mind and take a chance on a new course; being agile enough to move around for better angles or more light; and being quick to get packed and moving on an assignment.

In a fast-breaking news story, to get to the center of things and start taking pictures immediately is the ultimate goal. The quickness with which you can begin working and get to the heart of the action is crucial. You must work fast. You must be aware of what's happening; you can't timidly hang back. It takes practice and self-confidence to learn not to stand there and hope for the best. As John Loengard, picture editor of *Life* magazine, told me, "Photojournalism is not a genteel business."

In a feature story, don't get tied into doing things only one way. If the editors have already decided on the pictures they want and the pictures aren't working out, you've no time to waste or you'll lose the story. Your mind must be mobile. You must be quick to see when to change course, and be prepared to go in the opposite direction if necessary. Sometimes there are signs that alert you to the need for change. More often, a situation will arise so quickly that you have to move fast to catch it or stand there and watch the opportunity go by.

Moving around for different angles, better light, a different picture, I take for granted. Some photographers are apt to stand like a bunch of sheep for hours, telling each other jokes and talking shop, rather than give up their position. True, agencies like AP and UPI have assigned areas that they must cover, and their photographers are some of the best around, but generally, the only way to get a picture that no one else has is to move away from the crowd. Try never to run with the flock. Position yourself so that if you see an opportunity opening up in another area, you can get there fast. Moving to a different location at the last possible minute will ensure that you have the advantage to yourself.

I've seen photographers go out with so many cameras around their neck that they are unable to move. It's physically impossible to move around weighted down by too much heavy equipment. When you lose your agility, other photographers can outmaneuver you. It's amazing how many photographers I know who have back trouble. I'm sure it is from carrying too many cameras and heavy camera bags.

Not being weighted down is important in sustaining mobility, too. On the Meredith March in 1966 with Martin Luther King, Jr., walking in the hot sun all day, I began to feel the weight of the camera bag and started to think, "Well, I'll let that one pass; there will be other pictures," merely because I was too tired to move. Don't get weighted down into this type of situation.

I try to blend in with the surroundings. I want to be as unobtrusive as possible on reportage assignments, so the subject can carry on normally. I've taken my best pictures armed with two cameras and three extra lenses, a total of five lenses.

Assignments come up on a moment's notice and I must be prepared for them. Being able to pack and get going quickly is another kind of mobility. (In the past year, I have been on assignment in Africa, Japan, France, Spain, Tortola, Canada, West Germany, and Northern Ireland, and have crisscrossed the United States several times.) Being able to move quickly, with a passport and shots up to date, equipment in good repair, and sufficient rest to withstand jet lag and the sometimes less-than-comfortable conditions, is an absolute necessity.

To get pictures that are alive, moving, animated, it's important to be mobile—quick-thinking, quick-moving, quick-changing. I'm always aware that I must have mobility to get to the center, to the core, to the heart of the action. To capture the moments I want, mobility is essential.

Mrs. Martin Luther King, Jr., and her children were coming off the plane that carried her husband's body home to Atlanta for burial in 1968. I had left the photographers' area at the last minute to go down into the crowd of people waiting for them to arrive. They all came together in the doorway of the airplane for just a moment. Because they were in the shadows, I twisted the lens wide open and took one frame. In the next frame they were gone. It's a picture that I don't mind saying is mine. (200 mm)

It was the first round of the second heavyweight championship fight between Sonny Liston and Cassius Clay in Lewiston, Maine, in 1965. The fight had just started and I wanted to change a lens. I waited until what I thought was a lull, when Clay and Liston were a good bit apart. As I went into my bag for the lens, I heard a yell and looked up. The referee had started to count Liston out. It was the famous phantom-punch fight, when no one saw the blow that knocked out Sonny Liston. Clay looked warily at Liston while the bewildered referee, Jersey Joe Walcott, held up the winner's hand. (200 mm)

Cassius Clay, before he became Muhammad Ali, had just won the world heavyweight boxing title from Sonny Liston in Miami Beach in 1964. At the end of the sixth round I looked over at Clay's corner and could see joy coming into his face. It dawned on me that Sonny Liston was not going to make the bell and come out for the next round I moved around ringside to Liston's corner. When the referee walked over to Clay to hold up his hand, Clay was already moving away from him, leaping around the ring with his trainers. He jumped over to Liston's corner, diving around and shouting. (50 mm)

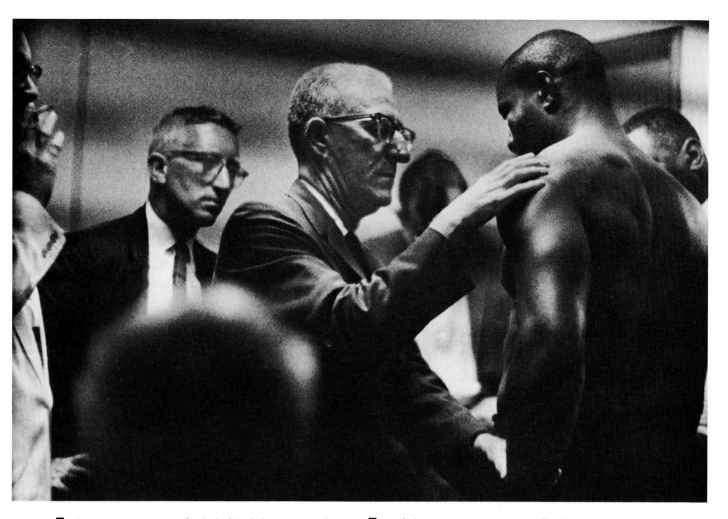

At a sports event, what's behind the action always interests me more than the action itself. After Sonny Liston failed to come out in the seventh round, I followed him to the hospital. I walked around the hospital looking in the windows and saw the doctors and boxing commission officials examining his shoulder, asking him questions, trying to determine if he had thrown the fight. I took this photograph of Liston through the venetian blinds. When they saw me they closed the blinds. (50 mm)

Muhammad Ali in his dressing room in Puerto Rico in 1976. He was going to fight Jean-Pierre Coopman in a world title fight. He knew he was the greatest, yet there was the apprehension of danger in his eyes.

Later that day, while photographing Don King, the fight promoter, around the swimming pool of the hotel where he was staying, I slipped and landed on my camera, breaking a rib. When I came to, Ali's doctor and his trainer, Angelo Dundee, were standing over me. I still covered the fight that night for *Sports Illustrated,* although every time I lifted my arms or turned quickly I felt terrible pain. Mobility barely entered my head; I was concerned with just getting through the night. (50 mm)

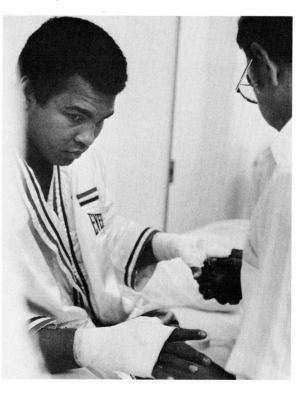

It was Weeb Eubanks's last season as head coach of the Jets. I was doing a photo essay on the team's entire season, the football season of 1973-74. When the story appeared in *New York* Magazine they had lost so many games and had so many injured players that it was titled "The Agony of a Losing Season."

I took just one quick frame of the team in the shower after they lost the second game against Buffalo I was watching for a moment that would not offend anybody. Because of the way each player was accidentally standing, this picture is completely inoffensive. Many pictures are a combination of luck and good timing. (35 mm)

When the team wins the pain is not so bad, but the Jets had just lost to the Houston Oilers in 1972, and quarterback Joe Namath sat in his stall for awhile plucking up enough courage to take the bandages and brace off his often-injured knees. I used an 85 mm lens so that I wasn't right on top of him. I wanted to show what his life was really like.

Bobby Kennedy was marching up Fifth Avenue on Saint Patrick's Day in 1968, the day he announced he was going to run for the presidency. As we marched, he turned, pointed his finger toward a building, and smiled. I followed his movement and there was Jackie Kennedy and John-John, leaning out of a window waving to him. He knew she would be there. (200 mm)

President Nixon campaigning for reelection in 1972. He was way ahead in the polls and decided to ride in an open car down the streets of Laredo, Texas. He received cheers from the people on the street and seemed to enjoy it. I was in the car ahead of him and jumped out because he was starting to work the crowd, shaking hands and generally giving his Secret Service men something to worry about. I had been traveling with the campaign and the Secret Service men knew who I was, so I was able to get as close as I wanted. Their eyes were fixed on the crowd. (24 mm)

French President Charles de Gaulle greeting French Canadians on his visit to Canada in 1967. He was a man who was usually aloof. This was the first time I'd ever seen him mingling with the people, the first time he exhibited what I call the common touch. I was surprised—security was tight because there had been an assassination threat made on his life earlier in the trip. (35 mm)

During a wine-tasting party in 1974 given by California's congressional delegation, I saw President Nixon's personal secretary, Rose Mary Woods, and her escort, Robert Gray, a Washington, D.C., advertising executive, slip outside and I followed them. They sat down on chairs just outside the reception area. I asked them if they would sit in front of the Capitol Building, a better background. Watching the daylight fade, they seemed to forget the Watergate scandal for a moment. (28 mm)

After a forty-eight-day trial in 1974 on charges of conspiring to block a federal investigation of fugitive financier Robert L. Vesco, former Attorney General John Mitchell and former Secretary of Commerce Maurice Stans were acquitted. After the verdict, Stans moved through the revolving doors of New York's courthouse into a crush of photographers and re-porters and said, "I feel reborn." I left my position near the doorway and quickly backed across the street, away from the other newsmen. It's almost a cliché of what a forties film might depict, but moving away actually helped capture the drama of the situation. This technique doesn't always work, so you are taking a calculated risk. (35 mm)

In this side view of The Who, there is drama in the crowd—you see their ghostly faces, their hands, the spotlight. It was taken for *People* during their concert tour in 1980. This was a difficult picture to get because the security guards didn't want anybody on the stage and The Who were afraid I might trip over their amplifiers. That would be a catastrophe, because if a rock group can't plug in, there's no music. I talked them into letting me up on the stage, and I'm pleased with the effect. (35 mm)

During a Mick Jagger and Rolling Stones concert at Madison Square Garden in 1968, I was shoved around a bit by hysterical fans trying to get to the stage. Just getting past all of them and the security guards was a chore. I went with only one camera and two lenses so I could move around and focus on the stage. (28 mm)

Photographing Paul McCartney during a Wings concert in Philadelphia in 1976, I maneuvered in and out of the security area to get the angle I wanted of him onstage. I let the security guards see my credentials for the event—a special Wings badge plastered on my jacket so that I could get back into the roped-off area again when I wanted to. I always try to let the security guards know who I am before leaving a security area so that I won't be kept out when trying to return. (85 mm)

After the concert I pushed quickly through the crowd to make certain I got backstage with him before the doors were locked. Backstage, he sat down, exhausted and sweating, but relaxed; he still looked as if he had had a good time. (50 mm)

I was in Antigua on holiday in 1976 when Greta Garbo swam past me. You can imagine my surprise. As a child just starting to go to the movies I used to hear my mother and father talk about the "great Garbo," and here she was in front of me, looking straight at me, into my camera, without her sunglasses on. I wasn't going to let the chance pass. I couldn't. (300 mm)

PHOTOGRAPHING PEOPLE

Personalities and famous people have always interested me, especially if they're known to be difficult. It challenges me. A major aspect of my photography is photographing and getting close to difficult people. It has taken me years of observing human behavior to figure out and anticipate how people will react to being photographed.

Most of the people I photograph are in the news. People in the news, those in the spotlight, are very much aware of their importance. I want to photograph people when they're at the center, at their best. To photograph Winston Churchill during the war or Joe Louis in his prime is a lot different from photographing them years later when they aren't at the center of things.

Busy, accomplished people have one thing in common—they don't have much time to be photographed —and many can be difficult to work with or even to get to. Having a prestigious magazine behind you is without a doubt an important persuader. My main purpose in this is to get as close to them photographically as possible in the amount of time I have. I want to show each person as he is, and not photograph everyone in the same way. I like to come in with new ideas for each person I photograph. Even if I come back the next day for a second take, I want to have fresh ideas. I want to hear that I have taken a good picture of someone, not that it looks like one I did a year ago. I've seldom taken a good picture of somebody without wondering later if anyone else could see what I was looking at. I think of what Robert Burns, the Scottish poet, said about "Oh wad some power the giftie gie us/ to see oursels as others see us!" I do not go in with the intention of being brutally telling: my purpose is to record what is there. You mustn't be too protective of your subjects. If they do something, it's your job to photograph it. The photographer is in a unique position of being the recorder of our times. I think a photographer can get a lot closer to people than most reporters can.

If someone is difficult to get to because of a busy schedule or because he's camera-shy, explain that the pictures will only take a few minutes of his time. When you arrive, explain right away that time is limited, then let him know what you'd like to do and what is needed for the story. Ask for more than you expect to get.

If you're overwhelmed by your famous subject, lulled into a kind of "this is wonderful" attitude and carried away by the person you're photographing— you'll be in trouble. Instead, take charge of the sitting, building up a rapport as you work. Watch the subject's mood as an indicator of how far you can go. Get the subject to open up, to reveal the real person behind the name, or some reasonable facsimile thereof.

Initially keep the conversation light. I'll talk about anything at all that will relax him and me—anything that is not offensive and won't jar him. I keep away from controversial subjects. After all, I'm not going to change his mind any more than he is going to change mine. If you've done your homework, you will have some idea of what to expect from even the most difficult of people.

Sometimes you have to orchestrate a picture; you can't always be satisfied with whatever someone is doing. Don't be afraid to suggest something because it's too outrageous—you never can tell. Be a director, making time work for you, full of ideas and fast to utilize the time you have. Let things happen, but also have everything quietly under control.

Be aware of how far you can push a subject. Watching the situation closely soon becomes second nature. Be aware of when to push and when to let up. It's always better for the subject to think afterward that he went too far than for you to realize that you didn't go as far photographically as you could have gone. Forget about making a new friend—the point is to get on with your work. Do a good, professional job and you'll be remembered.

Get your subjects to change clothes. A person's mood will change with what he has on. You'll see subtle changes in the photographs. You'll get a more diverse set of pictures with which a picture editor can work. Try to photograph people at home. The pictures are much more personal, and people love to look at the way other people live.

If the situation is going badly—a clash of personalities, or a reluctance to do anything you suggest—back off: don't continue in that vein. Start a new approach to try to salvage the day. Pushing after a point will not make the pictures any better, only worse.

Suggest a new picture situation near the end of a sitting, after the subject is relaxed and responsive. It's better to bore him for five minutes at the end than to have your inspiration while flying home over the Atlantic. Innocent oblivion to his restlessness keeps things going a little longer. When it's going well, don't stop; keep up the momentum. When it's good, keep going.

I've found that I actually photograph better when I have only a short time with someone, rather than plenty of extra time. The momentum and tension build up and the pictures have to be taken *now*. Part of my motivation comes from my Fleet Street days in London, working for the *Daily Express*. I remember all the times I had to stand outside Buckingham Palace knowing my picture opportunity would probably be the back of the royal heads driving away. A wave of the hand would make my day. From this experience I knew that if only I could have the chance to photograph an important person in his environment, his home, I would catch the moment. I would make every moment count.

Suffragist Alice Paul worked all her life for the women's movement. I photographed her in her Washington, D.C., home in 1970 for *Life*. I expected to find an old lady but instead found a feisty woman who was still having a great time working for her cause. (24 mm)

Edward Albee was working on turning the book *Lolita* into a stage play when this photograph was taken at his loft in New York City in 1980. He was a very sullen man, introspective, almost brooding. Trying to give the picture some warmth, I asked him to hold his cat. (Hasselblad, 85 mm)

In 1976 I photographed Truman Capote for *People*. He is so clever; he has an uncanny way of reading your mind. He knew I wanted good pictures, so he sat under a portrait of himself painted when he was thirty-five years old. He knew the contrast would be amusing. (First Place, Portraits, University of Missouri Pictures of the Year.) (28 mm, strobe)

The celebrities I photograph for *People* are the ones readers like to see and know more about. There is always a lot of reader reaction to the photographs. Here are a few taken backstage before the public image is turned on.

I photographed Margaux Hemingway when she first came to New York, before she became a model, when she was just a big, pretty girl from Idaho who said "scoo-bee-doo" a lot. By 1975 she had become more polished. (50 mm)

In 1970 I did a story on Johnny Carson for *Life*. I liked him. He was completely opposite from the way he appears on television. No one is exactly the way you think they are. Offstage, he's very private. He was just the way I want people to be with me, friendly and pleasant but not palsy-walsy. The photograph was taken backstage in a makeshift dressing room in Lubbock, Texas, where he was making a one-night appearance. Carson's son Ricky is in the background. (35 mm)

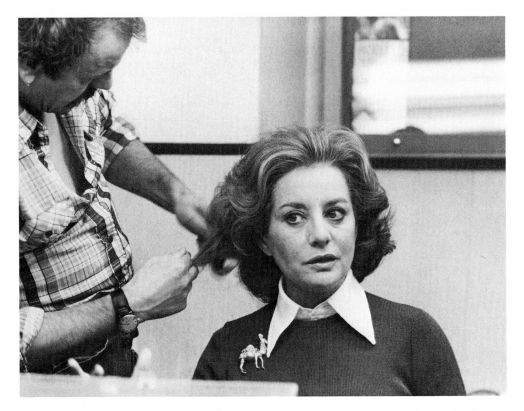

In 1976 when Barbara Walters was co-host of the *Today* show, backstage before the show began, she commented that her life was governed by washing and setting her hair and doing her makeup five mornings a week. There is tension in her face as she readies herself for her morning's work. (85 mm)

"I get this shivering feeling before I go on," Tammy Grimes told me in her dressing room at the Winter Garden Theatre, as the star of *Forty-second Street,* the biggest Broadway musical of the 1981 season, waited for her cue. She is very professional and knows what is needed to get a good picture story. If she agrees to something, she won't change her mind. She makes it easy to take a good picture. (85 mm)

Anthropologist Margaret Mead was a guest lecturer at the Choate School in 1969 when I photographed her for *Life*. "It's as simple as that," she seemed to gesture. She had spent her whole life telling people what she had learned and it was easy for her to speak in front of an audience. (200 mm)

During the summer of 1972 I read that the Health Department had asked Edith Bouvier Beale to clean up her mansion in the Hamptons on Long Island. I drove up to her house and knocked on the door. When her daughter, Edie, learned I was a Scot, she invited me in. The house was in a terrible state of neglect, cats and racoons all about. Edith, still a very handsome woman, came downstairs to pose in the living room beside a portrait of herself as a young woman. She told me she hadn't been downstairs in three years. Looking around, she told Edie that it was time she did some dusting. (24 mm)

Bobby Fischer completely mesmerized his Russian opponent, Boris Spassky, defeating him in the World Chess Championship in Iceland in 1972. To get to Fischer at that time and take pictures of him for *Life* was not the easiest of tasks. Bobby doesn't like being photographed and was having a bad time with the press. I've often thought there has to be one friend in the "enemy camp," and this time it was me. I had a lot of fun photographing him, mainly because I was doing something my collegues couldn't do.

At 5:00 A.M. Fischer was huddling in the back of a boat in a chilly fjord near Reykjavik. He liked to stay up all night and sleep all day. He put the blanket over his head and shoulders and sat alone in the back of the boat. (24 mm)

Overleaf: Some of my favorite pictures are the strange ones, such as Bobby Fischer being kissed by a horse outside Reykjavik. It fitted in with his isolation and idiosyncrasies that a horse would befriend him. This was a completely natural, spontaneous picture. (28 mm)

On Long Island in 1980, mother Teri Shields joked with daughter Brooke after the photography session was over. (35 mm)

Brooke with her father, Frank Shields, at his Long Island home in 1978. (28 mm)

I had seen Brooke Shields making this face for some of her friends and I asked her to do it for me. Her film *Pretty Baby* had just come out, and I was doing a story on her for *People* in 1978. I was tired of always seeing her made to be what she wasn't. I wanted to show what I had seen—a girl capable of clowning around like the youngster she was. (100 mm)

I was doing a cover story on fashion designer Halston for *People* in 1977. The only place I could get him together with two of his most famous clients, Liz Taylor and Liza Minnelli, was at Wolf Trap, an open-air theater near Washington, D.C. I improvised a studio by putting up the seamless paper in a locker room. (wide-angle Rolleiflex)

I liked the quiet, stoic way Phillip Rogers, twenty-two, of Freer, Texas, looked sitting at Camp Atterbury, Indiana. He had a good face. I took his picture because he had a haunted look. He was waiting to be pardoned under President Ford's amnesty program in October 1974. An infantryman in Vietnam for over two years when he deserted, he went home because his mother became ill. "Everybody knew I was AWOL," he said, "but they figured I had good reason." He even filed income tax returns every year and was not arrested. He turned himself in and was sentenced to eleven months alternative service. (Hasselblad, 150 mm)

Dolly Parton was looking into a full-length mirror, getting ready for me to photograph her. She said she would be ready for me in a minute. I answered, "Keep doing what you're doing, Dolly, because you're looking good." It was a completely spontaneous picture and by far the one I like best from that day in Nashville in 1976. (85 mm)

Lawyers must all be good actors. F. Lee Bailey likes an air of intrigue. At his desk in 1973 he gives the impression that he could handle any case. (35 mm)

Broadway producer Alexander Cohen shown in his office in the Shubert Theater in 1980. He believes in old-fashioned showmanship and pizazz and keeps a supply of candy in his office at all times. (35 mm)

Francis Bacon, one of Great Britain's foremost painters, was in New York for the opening of his exhibition at the Metropolitan Museum of Art in 1975. His paintings have faces of nightmares, anguished men, tortured humans. He was overseeing the hanging of his work, and he rested for just a moment during the arduous task. I had photographed him years ago in London, but the negatives are lost. I liked his honesty. (35 mm)

George C. Scott was making his directorial debut as well as starring in the movie *Rage* in 1972. Everyone on the set was aware of his famous temper, but I got on quite well with him. He came over and asked me to be in one of the last scenes of the film. He needed a photographer to run past a fire and photograph it. I found it excruciatingly embarrassing to have to stand there and then run "like a photographer" past a fire. He directed me in the scene and said it was really funny, but I think it was cut from the film before it was released. (50 mm)

Maureen Stapleton waiting backstage before going on in the Neil Simon play *The Gingerbread Lady* in 1971. She told me she is always afraid until she gets on stage. The photograph was taken while I was doing a story on Neil Simon for *Life*. I didn't want to get too close and disturb her so I used a 105-mm lens, and as the light was practically nonexistent I pushed the Tri-X film in developing from its normal 400 ASA to 1600 ASA.

In 1979 I was doing a story on Burt Reynolds when he visited his parents in Florida. His retired police chief dad and his mother, both in their seventies, live on a ranch there. They were very pleasant, and Burt seemed to enjoy visiting quietly with them on the porch. I prefer to photograph people in their own environment whenever possible—it gives me a better idea of what someone is like. Burt is a very private person, and I was pleased to get a family portrait. (85 mm)

Faye Dunaway had just completed her role as Joan Crawford in *Mommie Dearest* in 1981 when I photographed her with her own mother, Grace, who was visiting her in New York. (Minolta CLE range-finder, 28 mm)

Photographing Farrah Fawcett for the cover of *People* in 1981, I found that the longer we worked the more interesting the pictures became. This was her third change of clothes; we had saved the outfit we liked best for last. (Hasselblad, 150 mm, strobe)

I photographed author Alexander Solzhenitsyn for *Life* in 1981. It was the first time in his eight years of exile from Russia that he had allowed anyone to photograph him at his home in Vermont. (Photographer of the Year portfolio, University of Missouri Pictures of the Year, 1981) (28 mm)

When General Alexander Haig, Jr., retired as NATO's Supreme Allied Commander in 1979, there was speculation that he would run for president. I thought it appropriate to photograph him at the site of the Battle of Waterloo in Belgium. (24 mm)

In 1981 I photographed Tony Bennett in his New York apartment for the *New York Times Magazine* for a story on the return of fifties singing idols. (20 mm, strobe)

Disco owner Regine rests her feet in ice buckets after dancing all night at her club in Marbella, Spain. (First place, Portraits, University of Missouri Pictures of the Year, 1978) (85 mm, strobe)

New York City was on the verge of bankruptcy in 1975 when I met Mayor Abe Beame in the middle of the Brooklyn Bridge for a feature in *Life* magazine. (Hasselblad, 50 mm, hand-held flash)

Fashion designer Halston with his dog on the stairs of his Manhattan town house in 1978. (28 mm)

I photographed Paloma Picasso in Paris for the January 1981 issue of *Harper's Bazaar.* Framed in the window, she looked like one of her father's paintings. (85 mm)

A good picture doesn't necessarily generate newsstand sales. *People* used this picture of J. Paul Getty on one of their first covers in 1974. Though it was a disaster at the newsstand because Getty's face wasn't recognizable, it is still one of my favorite pictures. (85 mm)

I flew to Dallas, Texas, in 1980 to do a story on financier Bunker Hunt for *Life,* after reports that he had tried to corner the market in silver. (Hasselblad, 80 mm, strobe)

Richard Todd was about to take over as Jets quarterback for eleven-year-veteran Joe Namath in 1976. Todd and Namath had both played quarterback for the University of Alabama under coach Bear Bryant. I thought there was a striking resemblance between them. (135 mm)

On Bird Island, a small island in the Seychelles, on assignment for French *Vogue* in 1976, I suggested to Roman Polanski that he be photographed buried up to his neck in sand. He thought it was a smashing idea—until the tide came in. (35 mm)

I photographed William Holden and Stephanie Powers at home in California in 1977. He loved Africa and exotic animals and had, among other things, a boa constrictor that I photographed them with. But I wanted something else, some movement in the pictures. I had read that they loved to ride his motorcycle, so I asked them to ride around me in a circle while I followed them with the camera. I wanted to get away from the usual "celebrity-sitting-around-the-pool" picture. (135 mm)

Dennis Hopper and Peter Fonda wrote, produced, directed, and starred in *Easy Rider,* which has been called the definitive motion picture of the hippie generation. They were still living their part when I photographed them for *Vogue* in 1969. (35 mm)

I photographed Ronald and Nancy Reagan on his California ranch at Lake Malibou in November 1966, just before he was elected governor of California. (135 mm)

I like to step back to show the environment and place the subject in time. Edward Gorey, author, illustrator, set and costume designer, is seemingly amused by dark satire. Here, in 1978, he stands in his living room in the apartment he shares with five cats. (35 mm)

Dan Rather, CBS-TV newsman, was White House correspondent when this picture was taken in 1973. His running television battle with President Nixon during the Watergate investigation established his reputation as the journalist the Nixon White House hated the most. I don't usually go in so close on a person's face, but it seemed to best illustrate the story I was doing for *New York* Magazine. (35 mm)

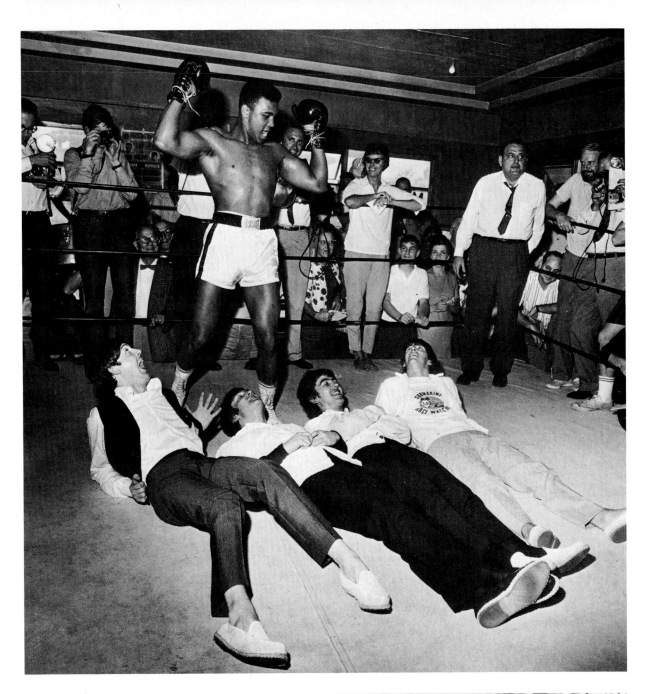

The Beatles were in Miami in 1964 and so was Cassius Clay, who was training for his world title fight with Sonny Liston. I had the idea of bringing the Beatles to see him, mainly because Liston was very difficult to get to and Clay was interested in publicity. Afterward the Beatles were furious, especially Lennon, who said, "We went to the wrong man. He made us look like chumps. He's going to be knocked out." For the next few days the Beatles were a bit cool to me, until Clay won the world title. (wide-angle Rolleiflex)

Ed Sullivan put on a Beatles wig for an instant before the Beatles came out to perform on his television show in New York in 1964. (35 mm)

Things were not always happy for the Beatles. During an interview in 1966 John Lennon said that the Beatles were more popular than Jesus. The consequences were enormous—people in the Bible Belt were burning Beatles records. Lennon sits alone in his Chicago hotel room shortly thereafter. (35 mm)

Overleaf: When photographing Fred Astaire and his wife, jockey Robyn Smith, at their home in California for *People* in 1981, I asked him to dance for me. The closest I got was when he crossed his legs in an elegant Astaire pose as she rode out of the picture. At eighty-one he still had "it." (Photographer of the Year portfolio, University of Missouri Pictures of the Year, 1981) (24 mm)

COMPETING UNDER PRESSURE

After photographing Henry Kissinger at the Paris Peace Talks in 1972, while the world waited to get in, I said, "Thank you, Mr. Secretary, for giving me this exclusive for *Life* magazine." He paused, looked up and smiled, and said something like "I think you got some good pictures." He didn't tell me it was going to be an exclusive; I gave *him* the idea. *Time* magazine later asked to photograph him, but the reply was that the pictures had been promised exclusively to *Life*.

Competition is what it's all about. A good photojournalist competes with everybody—with other photographers and with himself as well. I am always trying to better a previous picture or improve on an assignment. Photojournalists must choose between socializing and competing with other photographers. There is always a friendly rivalry among colleagues, a competitive camaraderie. If I have an exclusive, I'm not going to share it out of friendship, and neither would any good photojournalist. I worked too hard to get the picture.

It doesn't feel good to be scooped. I was looking for Sir Francis Chichester when he was circling the globe alone in a sailboat in 1966. He was rounding Cape Horn at the time. I rented a small plane and flew over Cape Horn for hours and hours in the most unbelievably bad weather I'd ever seen. The plane pitched back and forth in the turbulence. We refueled three times and flew out again, but we never found him. Back at the hotel, completely exhausted, I had just sat down when a batch of cables were brought in from the *Daily Express* in London. The last one was on top and read: THE PARTY'S OVER, BABY. REBASE IMMEDIATELY. WE HAVE BEEN SCOOPED BY THE *TIMES* OF LONDON AND THE BBC. IT WILL BE A LONG TIME BEFORE WE LIVE DOWN THIS DISGRACE. SIGNED, DAVID ENGLISH, FOREIGN EDITOR. As I read the other cables I could follow the hysteria backward to the first cable, which was simply: HOW ARE THINGS TODAY IN CHILE? It turned out that Sir Francis had given a fix on his position to the *Times* and the BBC—prearranged in London before he left. It didn't make it any easier for us. When you're beaten, you're beaten, but you can't tell that to the readers of the paper.

Sometimes you literally must outwait the other photographers to get the pictures you want. Never lose your determination—it pays off. Besides the physical stamina to sustain you over long hours of waiting or photographing with no letting up, a little ingenuity never hurts.

When I work with a reporter on a story, there is an uneasy truce between us. The competition is obvious—more pictures means less room for words. When the reporter makes the picture arrangements with the subject I am sure there will be some foul-up. The reporter can't help but take up most of the allotted time, and he wants to slant the pictures to fit the story he has in mind. When I was starting out, the reporter often presumed he was in charge of the story. Today, if a reporter tries to tell me what pictures to take, I listen, and if possible try to oblige, but the one picture I must bring back has got to come from me. With only a short time to get the subject relaxed enough to work with, I want as little interference as possible.

Considering the number of photographers covering major news stories, it's amazing that only two or three are able to function when disaster strikes. To be a real photojournalist, you must be able to compete, to keep working while horrendous events are going on all around you—be it a war, a riot, an assassination, a plane crash, or a fire. These situations are harrowing and extremely stressful. There is the *time pressure*, the immediacy of the situation: the split second in which you have to react, to get the camera up to your eye and start taking pictures. Your reaction must be completely spontaneous. There is the *emotional pressure* of being in the middle of a crisis, the horror of seeing a tragedy happening before your eyes. Because of the extreme stress, there is a tendency to break down emotionally, but you must be able to remain detached while recording for history what is going on around you. You must also contend with the *physical pressure,* the strain of being pushed and shoved, of having your own life endangered, and of coping with exhaustion.

To keep working during such turmoil you must remain calm and removed from the emotion of the event while at the same time recording it. Block out all extraneous chaos. Set your mind on your goal of bringing back the pictures. The camera will act as a buffer between you and reality. Keep thinking, "Capture the drama, capture the moment."

Since I first began thinking myself a photojournalist, I knew the day would come when I would be present at a terrifying event. I often thought about how I would react, and it worried me. The situation arose when Bobby Kennedy was shot in front of me. I kept saying, "This is for history. This is what I'm in the business for. Keep working at a 30th wide open." (A 30th being the speed at which I can hold a camera steady in bad artificial light.)

When it happened my reaction was "Every picture I've ever taken before can be destroyed as long as I get pictures here. It's too important, it's out of my hands, it's for the archives, for posterity." Although you've seen that image a hundred times on TV, it's gone just like that without a photograph to look at.

These situations are difficult because they're so harrowing. There are the crowds to worry about, the screaming, the police, the gunfire, and there are technical points to contend with, too. Don't let any kind of feeling you have for the person influence you. A photographer I spoke to afterward said he could not do it—it wasn't dignified, it was unethical, it lacked integrity. To me these are all just excuses for not being able to work under stress. I'm not there to editorialize about whether it is polite to photograph. I am there to record the event for history.

A photojournalist must be prepared for competition—to compete with other photojournalists, to compete with yourself for the one incredible picture that will never be repeated.

Henry Kissinger called his bedroom in the U.S. ambassador's residence in Paris "my battle station." The situation was extremely tense, as President Nixon had promised peace in Vietnam and Kissinger was burdened with negotiating it. (24 mm)

I had been trying to photograph "Papa Doc" Duvalier, president of Haiti, but to no avail. One afternoon I was told that there was no chance of photographing him at all. By the time I returned to my hotel room the phone was ringing to tell me I could see Papa Doc at five o'clock that same day.

When I walked into his office I instantly believed the stories I had heard. He was a very eerie-looking man. I could see his ivory-handled pistols on the desk. Although he was pleasant and autographed his book for me, he looked at me menacingly, as a boxer looks at his opponent. Later, looking at the book he had given me, I saw that he had reproduced my photograph of Mrs. Martin Luther King, Jr., without permission, in his book. (28 mm)

On trial in Haiti in 1968, British subject John Knox was accused of spying. His defense was that he had come to Port-au-Prince for plastic surgery. I had a Tonton Macoute (Haitian secret service man) as a chauffeur, and he never left my side. I got the feeling that he wasn't merely a chauffeur when he marched into the Haitian attorney general's office without knocking. The irony of it all was that they would let me photograph *inside* the courtroom, but not outside.

Knox *(right)* was convicted and later given clemency by Duvalier. (85 mm) The photograph *(below)* shows banana republic justice, with the lawyers drinking beer in the courtroom. (50 mm)

It was extremely hot in Philadelphia, Mississippi, in 1966, the day after we had all been tear-gassed on the Meredith March. Taking his jacket off because of the heat, Martin Luther King, Jr., slung it over his shoulder and kept going. It had been a bad scene the night before, with tear gas going off all around us, women and children screaming, and the police beating the marchers with batons. (135 mm)

No one had been allowed to photograph President Jimmy Carter on *Air Force One.* I knew he was going to fly to New York to give a speech after I finished photographing him in the Oval Office. The session went well, and I asked Jody Powell if there would be an opportunity for me to take pictures on the plane. I pointed out that it would be a shame not to get more pictures for *Life.* Powell told me to meet him after the speech and I'd fly on *Air Force One.*

It was the time in 1979 when Carter was very low in the polls and Ted Kennedy had hinted at his candidacy. Returning to Washington after a hard day of campaigning in New York, Carter showed the strain for just a second, putting his hand up to his forehead. Even though the picture is not quite in focus, it tells the story better than the others I took that day. It was the one that captured the mood I wanted. (24 mm)

In May 1965, during the civil war in the Dominican Republic, I was captured by both sides in one day. Rebel guns were pointed into the car in which I was riding, and I was marched away amid cries of "American spy." My Scottish accent got thicker and thicker as I explained who I was. After being released, I was seized by the police, again at gunpoint. I was searched and made to stand against the wall with my arms up while guns were waved around my head. Walking down the middle of the street during the fighting was probably the most stupid and dangerous thing I have ever done. (28 mm)

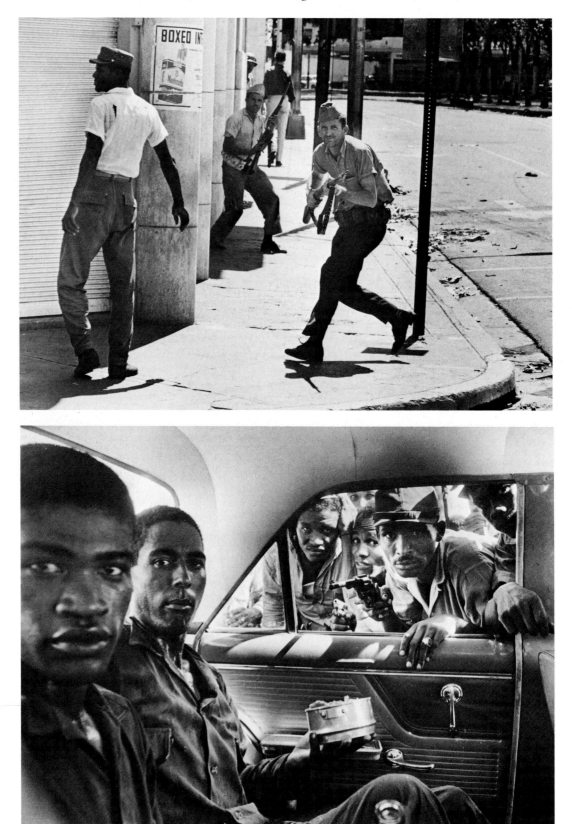

The subject of a 1975 feature in *People,* U.S. Marshal John Partington's job is to protect, relocate, and provide a completely new identity for those who turn state's evidence. Working quickly, Partington (*right*) with the help of state troopers with submachine guns, rushes a Mafia informer from a helicopter in Providence, Rhode Island, to a waiting car. The risk is always that there might be a leak in security; therefore they are extremely cautious. (24 mm)

In 1980 Camille Bell stands outside the abandoned E. P. Johnson School in Atlanta, Georgia, where her murdered son, Yusaf, was found. She told me she would never go to his gravesite until the murderer was caught. She just couldn't bear it. A very articulate woman, she became a leader in organizing to try to find the mass murderer of the Atlanta children. (24 mm)

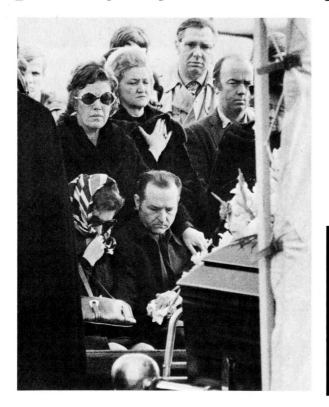

In 1972, George Diener, a Long Island food salesman, killed his seventeen-year-old son, Richie, for allegedly attacking him while in a drug-induced rage. Mr. and Mrs. Diener had agreed to let *Life* do a story on them. After I arrived at Long Island National Cemetery for the funeral and started photographing, things got tense. Someone came over and wanted to know who I was and why I was there, so I left, but not until I'd taken this picture with a 200-mm lens.

In 1964 in the village of Ghaziveran, Cyprus, this Turkish couple had just identified a young man killed in battle a few hours earlier as their relative. British soldiers were trying to comfort the grief-stricken pair. The nearby battle was between the Turks of Ghaziveran and the Greek Cypriots. Not permitted to take part in the fighting, the British soldiers were allowed only to help with the dead and wounded and comfort the survivors. (24 mm)

Being inside the limosine with the Beatles gave me another look at what life was like for them. I was always amazed that no one was seriously hurt, because as we went through the crowds I could hear thuds and bangs and screams. This picture was taken during the first Beatles' visit to America in 1964 as they left the Plaza Hotel in New York. (35 mm)

It was a blustering cold day in New York City in 1980 when the Central Park memorial to John Lennon took place. I walked over from my apartment to photograph it because I had been with them in the beginning. I thought about all of John's first impressions of and wisecracks about New York. (24 mm)

I was standing on a chair to get some pictures of Senator Robert Kennedy after he won the presidential primary in California in 1968. He started to squeeze his way through the crowd toward the kitchen exit of the Ambassador Hotel. Then came the pistol shots and almost instant bedlam.

I was kicked and pummeled in the panic that broke out. My jacket was ripped. I saw several men not just weeping but being sick. Girls and women were crying hysterically. The noise was deafening; it seemed like everyone was screaming.

Bobby lay on the floor, and the crowd pressed toward him. His wife, Ethel, finally got to him. She knelt beside him, and the words I heard were: "Oh, I'm with you, my baby." She was not crying. Bobby was conscious. There was a little blood at his mouth and some on his chest. As she spoke, he looked up and forced a faint smile. Then his eyes glazed over.

"Get a stretcher," said someone. "Get two," another voice said, and then: "We need three. Get three." I saw then that Bobby was not the only one who was wounded. It was maybe two minutes before a policeman came into the corridor. I saw him load the shotgun he was carrying.

"Where's the ambulance?" a man shouted. Bobby was still lying there, with a black rosary that someone had given him lying on his chest. A man bent over him. I didn't know if he was a priest administering the last rites. At last the stretcher came and Bobby was carried out. Ethel was right behind.

On the floor was a pool of blood. A young woman placed her artificial straw boater beside it. At least some of the ugliness of the scene was hidden. (First place, News, British Press Pictures of the Year, 1968) (victory speech, 200 mm; Kennedy's face, 35 mm; Ethel Kennedy's hand, 35 mm; blood, 50 mm)

ESSAYS & SEQUENCES

The photo essay is an important aspect of photo-journalism and consists of a series of pictures that tell a story. A picture sequence is much like a photo essay in that it tells a story, but a sequence is much more fragmented. It's a vignette, whereas a photo essay tells a more complete story.

A sequence is frame following frame, possibly from a single roll of film, to present a slice of life. There must be a bit of drama in it—tragedy or humor, happiness or sadness. It's a piece of the whole. Many times you don't set out to do a sequence; it just happens and you capture it. You set out purposely to do a photo essay.

A photo essay might take place over a period of time, like the pictures of the Shock-Trauma unit, while a picture sequence, like the Robert Kennedy assassination, occurs as a single, brief event. Photo essays are difficult to do because a good photo essay must have three different kinds of pictures.

There is always one pivotal picture, the one that the whole story will be remembered by. I call it the glue that holds the story together. Every photo essay needs one great photo, one pivotal picture.

In addition to the pivotal picture, there is the lead picture, or opener. This is the first picture in the series and is a difficult one because it must provoke a reader's interest. Without a good opener, it is hard to get a reader's attention, but sometimes a photojournalist doesn't know what the opener will be until the story is laid out.

The final element in a photo essay is the incidental, or point, pictures. These pictures help move the story along, adding information and drama. The point pictures are the backup, the support for the opener and the pivotal pictures.

What I love best about doing photo essays is the total freedom of selecting scenes to photograph. It takes a lot of hard work to bring back a photo essay that really tells a complete story, but it's worth the effort.

In New Orleans to photograph him for *People* in 1980, I had dinner with Truman Capote in the hotel where we were staying. The conversation came around to his book *In Cold Blood*. This sequence of photographs of Truman beginning to cry was taken while he explained how the two convicted murderers in his book told him that he was the only person who had ever loved them. (28 mm)

Zsa Zsa Gabor and Michael Paul, a Russian emigré oilman, were having a tête-à-tête at a Palm Beach party. This sequence is from a story on Palm Beach society that I did for the first issue of *People,* in 1974. Oblivious to the camera, Zsa Zsa held her companion captive while he amused her by reading her palm and telling her what seems to have been a very interesting bit of gossip. They laughed together like kids on a first date. (50 mm)

Opposite: I photographed student tutors from Mountain View High School in Mesa, Arizona, for a *Life* photo essay in 1981. *Above:* I wanted to show them actually tutoring (28 mm), and (*far right*) give an idea of the atmosphere at the school (85 mm). *Right:* I had T-shirts made for all of the tutors for a group photograph. (135 mm)

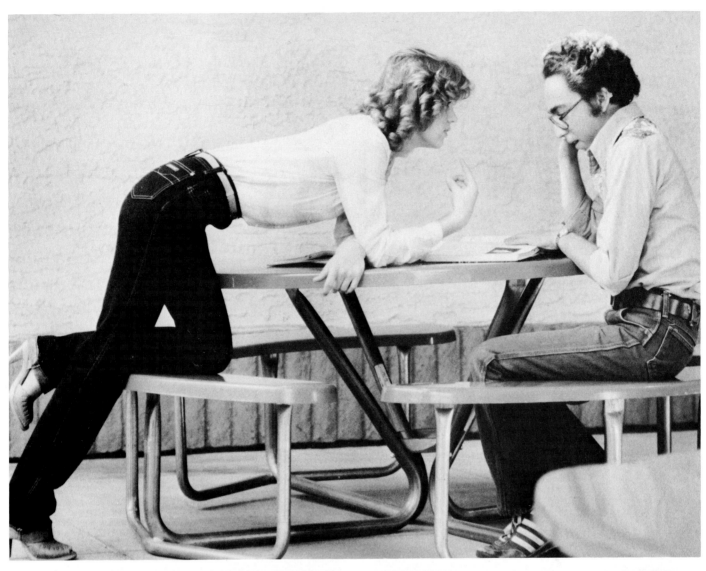

Janet Tanner, an executive for Aetna Life Insurance, was the subject of a 1981 photo essay for *Life*. I traveled with her for four weeks from Connecticut, Japan, and Florida on business to Tortola on holiday.

In a photo essay a number of pictures are necessary to get your point across. You must have an office picture if you're dealing with an executive, but you must also have a change of pace, varying the mood of the story slightly while trying to give a complete picture of what her life is about.

Photography: Harry Benson
Reporting: Margot Dougherty

In mid-meeting, Tanner consults with protégé Sharin Mathews, 25.

A WOMAN EXECUTIVE
REACHES FOR
POWER AT THE TOP

What Makes Janet Tanner Tick?

Janet Tanner, 36, is a nonstop, hard-driving and driven $60,000-a-year executive. As the highest-ranking woman in her division of Aetna Life and Casualty Insurance of Hartford, Conn., she is charged with the investment of $600 million a year. Her day starts at 5:30 a.m. and her commitment to work—both for Aetna and her own projects in real estate—is headlong and unceasing, like an obsessive love affair. She loves to negotiate, to manipulate, to thread her way toward the successful completion of a deal. Yet for all her ambition and toughness in a man's world, she occasionally takes cookies or a poem she's written to the office to bring some relief to a pressure-packed day. She's very much a creature of her competitive environment, shaping it and shaped by it, right down to the grey flannel suit she wears as a symbol of her growing power within the staid corporate establishment.

CONSTANT MEETINGS,
INCESSANT TRAVEL
AND
SNOWBALLING SUCCESS

Tanner whirlwinds through meetings, lunches in the male-dominated dining room and travels to inspect investments (right).

After a.m. jogging she mixes a brew of OJ and vitamins.

When Janet Tanner entered Columbia University's graduate program in business administration, in 1969 intent on being "the best securities analyst in the world," only 677 women in the U.S. got master's degrees in business. In 1980, when she was already the top woman in Aetna's financial division, 12,332 women earned the same degree. Still, Tanner's salary, according to the latest data, is matched or bettered by less than 1 percent of the total female work force. In fact, just 1.5 percent, earn $25,000 or more—all of which underscores her achievement in a field still sparsely populated by women.

Tanner is a big woman, 5 feet 9 and sturdily built. Her gait is strong, there's no wobble in the high heels that emphasize her commanding presence. Before work—and after a jog, a megadose of vitamins and a pill called Brittvom's Insurance Formula—she rips off to her famous 2902 to check the building she and her partners in a private venture have converted to office space. By 7:00 a.m. she's at Aetna, a half hour before other employees. "I'm not the insurance company type," she says. After 10 years with Aetna. "But if you want to move around big bucks, you've got to be in a big setting like this."

Tanner keeps an eye on 170 projects, including radio stations, timber, a dye plant, a skiwear firm, a paper plant in Alabama, an oil refinery in California. Her desk is clean (a friend advised her that a clean desk denotes a powerful executive) except for a still life of three autumn leaves, an ornamental box, a crystal dish and a brass paper-clip holder. Her day is a series of meetings. With small talk Tanner adeptly eases clients into spells about why Aetna should want to invest in their projects. She's also quick to ask tough questions, her calculator and pen poised, her eyes piercing. At a meeting where two men wanted money for a black-affairs television program, Tanner scrutinized their proposal, admired their entrepreneurship and suggested a loan of $30,000. "Thirty to sixty thousand is nothing," she said later in an aside. "When you get to a million, that's worth talking about.

She adores making deals, but on off-hours tries to check herself. "On weekends I go to the farmers' market and find myself negotiating over a lousy artichoke. If you're not careful, you find yourself negotiating with friends I don't want that."

Tanner was married for eight years and has been divorced for seven. "I liked being married," she says, eschewing details. Then she adds firmly, "I like being single." Her father, 70, has a consulting firm. Her mother is a librarian. Tanner also writes poetry and regards as her spiritual adviser Nell Dorr, an 89-year-old photographer whose picture of a mother and child hangs in Tanner's apartment and whose homilies sprinkle her speech. "The life of courage is the life to lead" is often heard. "I figure I have about four lives going at once," she says. "If I'm putting seventy percent at each, I'm living a wonderful life. But if I had children and I were giving only seventy percent to a child, that's no good."

She does give a lot of time to the six people who report to her, especially her protégé Sharin Mathews, 25, who has worked for her for two years. He says of her, "Sometimes she just goes too fast or takes something too personally. But she'll always give you your ten minutes." If Tanner feels any special pressures because she's such a high-ranking woman at Aetna, she doesn't show it. "I am not a hard-core women's libber," she says. "But I'll change my own tires, I don't want to be anybody's shadow."

Back from a trip, she tells her boss of the successful venture.

Tanner soaks in an ofuro (left), jokes with Zen-Noh's boss (above) and kneels at a tea ceremony with his daughter. Tanner understood the young woman to say that she was looking for a husband and replied, "Me too," provoking a round of giggles.

IN JAPAN THEY JOKED THAT SHE WAS 'MRS. AETNA'

Tanner recently represented Aetna in a $20 million investment arrangement with Zen-Noh, Japan's largest food co-op. Her job there was to size up grain silos, inspect produce markets and ask pointed questions. Finding themselves head to head with a full-steam-ahead woman executive—a species unknown in their country—came as a surprise to the Japanese executives. Ultimately the gentlemen were impressed. They were amazed to learn, however, that Tanner was not married. "Your husband is Mr. Aetna?" suggested a young man, who was familiar with American ways.

89

WHEN SHE ISN'T ON THE JOB, SHE'S HARD AT WORK ON PROJECTS OF HER OWN

Tanner horses around with James Wilkey and his daughter and more on a Caribbean beach. Before that Vietnam resort, she spends a day in the country with designer friend Kitty Daly and her daughter, Meg.

Tanner doodles a $1.3 million personal deal on a napkin as nightcap to a long, meeting-filled day.

At 7 a.m. Tanner studies plans at her converted factory.

During her "leisure" time Tanner works on real-estate development projects—for recreation. She and two male partners have converted an old factory into a building that has federal offices among its tenants. Tanner is concerned with every detail (Japanese cherry trees—her idea—dot the grounds). She is as likely to be found handing bricks to the bricklayer as tapping data into her ever-present calculator. She rarely sees her man of the moment, James Wilkey, 36, an IBM executive, and when he was recently transferred to Ohio, Tanner was a bit relieved; she won't have to consider "giving it all up to iron shirts." For slivers of time Janet Tanner can play in a carefree way, even consider motherhood and domestic life. But then she's back on the track, with little room for such concerns. If she is torn, the feeling is given low priority in the orderly, goal-oriented scheme of her life.

135

Before her 1971 wedding to Ed Cox, Tricia Nixon showed her father the correct way to offer his arm to walk her down the aisle as they entered the White House Rose Garden. She breathed a sigh of relief when he did it correctly. The pictures were laid out for inclusion in a story on her wedding that I did for *Life* but were taken out at the last minute because of lack of space. (50 mm)

President Richard Nixon riding with President Anwar El Sadat in a motorcade in Alexandria, Egypt, during Nixon's state visit in 1972. (85 mm)

The shah of Iran and his dog, Beno, at his villa on the Caspian Sea just before his empire crumbled in 1978. Earlier in the day Beno had prevented me from moving by placing his paw on my foot. One quiet word from the shah and the dog moved away. (28 mm, strobe)

For a 1980 *Life* essay on the Shock-Trauma unit of the University of Maryland, I wanted to show the tension of the emergency room. I followed the accident victims from helicopter to emergency and operating rooms where the Shock-Trauma team worked with precision and immediacy to save their lives. (*above*, 28 mm); (*right*, 85 mm)

For *Life* magazine in 1981 I photographed American doctor Eric Avery on his dawn rounds at Las Dhure, Somalia, where thousands of refugees arrive daily from war-torn Ethiopia. The first night I said to Dr. Avery, "Wake me at five." He said, "Don't worry, you'll be awake." He was right. The chanting and moaning of the starving children never stopped. (Photographer of the Year portfolio, University of Missouri Pictures of the Year, 1981) (105 mm)

This little girl had tuberculosis. She weighed less than 15 pounds although she was three years old. (35 mm)

Overleaf: While doing an essay for *Life* in 1980 on the drug epidemic among the young, I photographed these teen-agers on New York City's Lower East Side in a "shooting gallery," an abandoned room where they can get a fix while someone stands guard. I was actually photographing when a police raid occurred. (50 mm, tripod)

141

I photographed inside the maximum security area at Riker's Island prison in New York in 1981 for *New York* Magazine. The guard who escorted me was apprehensive about being there because of the possibility of being taken hostage. (Photographer of the Year portfolio, University of Missouri Pictures of the Year, 1981) (28 mm, tripod)

Russian President Leonid Brezhnev was in Washington, D.C., in 1973 for a state visit. Brezhnev seemed to spot me as he was coming down the stairs for a state dinner with President and Mrs. Nixon. His mood changed as he came nearer, and as a joke he came right up to the camera. It was a sequence I never expected to get, but using a motorized camera made it easy. (28 mm)

DEVELOPING A STYLE

Style is the individualized way in which to create drama or illustrate a point. Each photographer has a unique eye; use yours to create your own style. Don't be afraid to photograph things as you see them. Developing a style is an evolutionary process: the more you photograph, the more a style will emerge. A style takes time to develop, and it changes with your point of view.

Looking at photographs is useful in understanding style and technique. Studying other photographers for ideas, but not copying them, is extremely difficult. Trace a photographer's work and you can see whose style had an impact on it. Hardly anything is totally original—it's what a photographer does to expand on what has already been done that can make him an original in his own right. It's important to follow your own instincts.

Style becomes boring if it's too predictable—all the pictures begin to look alike. Don't be afraid to experiment with new techniques, new ways of doing things. Even if it turns out to be a disaster, learn from the mistakes and keep going. Be open to change, but don't accept trends without questioning their validity and usefulness for you.

When I say that getting as close as possible to a subject photographically is part of my style, I don't mean that I take extreme close-ups. One reason is that people don't look natural. Another reason I don't like them is that there is no frame of reference—they could have been taken anytime in the past thirty years. The big trouble when working in a studio is placing the person in time. If you step back a little, the mystery starts to unfold.

Cropping a negative to give the picture more of an impact or a different dramatic effect or to fit a page layout doesn't bother me. A photojournalist doesn't have the luxury of a still-life photographer, in which the situation remains static while he frames exactly what he wants. Continuous motion is essential to photojournalism and framing a picture can be difficult, so cropping can sometimes help.

While many photographs are a captured moment, totally spontaneous, there are also orchestrated pictures. These pictures have to be manipulated and directed by the photographer. The situation in between, which I call the controlled candid, is a re-creation of what the subject would normally be doing.

In a totally directed photograph, depending on the situation and the subject, I sometimes push for what would not normally occur. To capture a moment I want I will create a scene somewhat as a film director would. I see nothing wrong with it, especially with movie stars. I'm trying to take interesting pictures and they are trying to keep their images alive.

In controlled candids I'm not orchestrating so much. I reconstruct over and over what the subject would normally do until I get the results I want. I let the subject be himself, giving a little encouragement, while anticipating what he will do.

The totally spontaneous moments in which you have no control are, for example, hard news events or live concerts on stage—fleeting moments that you must capture. These moments won't be repeated, so the photojournalist's job is to select the moment to photograph, deciding what to capture and what to let pass.

Every photographer will achieve a style whether he wants to or not. It's one of the most dangerous things, because it is what all your pictures will eventually show, meaning all your pictures will start to look alike.

I try not to make my photography repetitive. I strive to take photographs that fascinate me. If you continue to change, to develop your style and expand your techniques, if you continually try new approaches, you're going to interest others.

Marshall McLuhan was a very dramatic person who liked to say dramatic things to get attention. I wanted a different picture, so I put a flash on my wide-angle Rolleiflex and asked him to put his hand on his head. He said he'd do better than that—he would salute me. The picture was taken in 1976 at the University of Toronto, where he had taught for thirty years.

Paul McCartney was improvising a little song at the piano for his three-year-old daughter, Stella, in 1975 in Los Angeles. She sat spellbound by her father's playing and singing.

I like the picture of Paul and his daughter because it is one of the few quiet, serious pictures I have ever taken of him. He is usually laughing or joking around, but here was a tranquil moment as he played for her. I like the contrast between his public and his private lives. (35 mm)

It was September 1975, school had just opened, and I was in Louisville, Kentucky, to photograph Mayor Harvey Sloane. He was trying to keep order in his city while enforcing the court-ordered busing of school-children between Louisville and the nearby suburbs.

After the pressures of a hard day, Mayor Sloane shares a quiet moment with his four-year-old daughter, Abigail. (50 mm)

Henri Langlois, founder of the Cinématique in Paris, is revered by the movie industry for having saved thousands of films that otherwise would have been lost. A longtime friend was visiting Langlois in his New York hotel room when this picture was taken for *Life* in 1971. Langlois was in America looking for more films for his Cinématique. (35 mm)

You must always have the straightforward picture if you're doing reportage, but for a different look I like back views, which offer a new perspective. It helps if the person is recognizable, like Bella Abzug, who was speaking here at a women's rally in New York in 1975. (24 mm)

In Omaha, Nebraska, in 1981, television exercise show host Richard Simmons jumped on the stage and shouted to the crowd who had come to see him "Do what I do" and immediately they did. You must never be faint-hearted or feel embarrassed if you think there is a picture in what you're doing. In order to get the effect I wanted I had to stand no more than two feet from him, which meant the camera was right down his throat and could have been annoying to him. I hadn't yet met him; this was our first contact as I had just gotten off a plane and driven straight to the rally already in progress. (20 mm)

I heard the Reverend Sun Myung Moon was going to have a meeting at some mansion. It was October 1975. I got up early, about 5:00 A.M., to follow him and his entourage to upstate New York for a rally in a rented meadow. His bodyguards didn't like my being there, but they let me in after I talked to them for a while. I wanted to photograph him speaking to all those innocent middle-class faces, enraptured by what he was saying. (20 mm)

153

After an early morning jog along the East River in 1981, New York Mayor Ed Koch reads the morning paper in his bedroom in Gracie Mansion. I saw the shadow across his eyes, which allowed him to read without turning his back on the sun. I thought of asking him to move but didn't because I thought the picture was more interesting the way it was. (24 mm)

For a *Life* magazine special issue, "A Day in the Life of America," in 1974, my assignment was Henry Kissinger, secretary of state at the time. Kissinger was holding his wife Nancy's hand in the back of his limousine, a private moment at the end of a long day. With only natural light and fast black-and-white film I got the gist of it, who they were, even in the dark car. I was not intruding. I was allowing them to carry on with their conversation without interrupting or saying anything to make them ill at ease. I was as unobtrusive as possible, and they almost forgot I was there. I had expected several pages in the issue, but this was the only picture *Life* used. (35 mm)

In 1964 in their suite at the George V Hotel in Paris, I asked the Beatles to compose something while I photographed them. My idea was to photograph them actually writing music—I wanted something real—and they complied. I moved in for a tight angle on Paul's and John's hands, for another look at them composing. (wide-angle Rolleiflex)

Feminist Germaine Greer was in New York in April 1971 to promote her book *The Female Eunuch,* and I was photographing her for *Life.* Here she was watching herself on a television talk show, in her room at the Chelsea Hotel in lower Manhattan, with a friend cuddled in front of her. She was totally absorbed by what she was saying on television— amused by it all. (50 mm)

It couldn't have been worse scheduling, Johnny Carson had been booked to play Lubbock, Texas, in January 1970, opposite the biggest football game of the season. Half the town was away at the match.

During rehearsals, I asked if he would walk back into the auditorium. He knew what the empty seats represented —but he gave me the picture anyway. (35 mm)

I was looking for a really dramatic setting for Peter Townsend of The Who as we were walking around Vancouver, British Columbia, before one of his rock concerts in 1980. It was Sunday and the railway yards were closed. We jumped over the tracks, and I told Peter to stand between the railway cars. (20 mm)

I wasn't surprised to find that comedian Steve Martin takes himself very seriously. I photographed him in Vail in 1978 with his cat and again in 1980 in Los Angeles, with another cat. He is very loyal to his cats. I brought the same element from one picture to the next, with different results. (*above,* Hasselblad, 80 mm) (*below,* 85 mm)

In Scotland in 1957 to open a new coal mine, Queen Elizabeth dressed for the occasion. (Speed Graphic)

Dr. Michael Ramsey, the archbishop of Canterbury, was visiting Las Vegas in September 1967. He is not being handcuffed and led away, as it appears, but is being helped with his robes by an obliging policeman. Earlier I had asked him to try a one-armed bandit. At the last minute he stopped; his hand was about one inch from it. Although it would have made a good picture, he realized it wouldn't further his career. (50 mm)

FROM STREET TO STUDIO

One minute I'm on the second floor of the White House, in a few hours I'm working on a cover photograph of Brooke Shields in the studio, and a little later I'm on the streets watching kids shoot heroin. It may sound glamorous and exciting, but there is a lot of frustration. Mainly, it's just hard work and waiting, waiting for the right assignment.

I can say now that I'm just as keen as when I started out. Just as apprehensive, just as insecure, just as excited at the prospect of taking pictures. I like the challenge of not knowing what lies ahead. I know I'm going to have some winners, some failures. I go all out while I'm doing an assignment because I remember the idle moments. I like the challenge of going into every area of photography, trying everything, even if it means leaving myself open to failure. The point is, the range of things a photographer can do is limitless.

I spend more time thinking about the assignment before I go out to do it than I used to. I wish I could go back and photograph some people and situations over again knowing what I know now. At times I wish I'd had a better sense of humor instead of being so heavy and serious; at others, I wish the pictures had been more serious instead of funny or gimmicky.

My photography has undergone an evolution of sorts over the years. I've refined certain aspects of my work, bringing what I've learned from one situation to the next. I've become more selective about when to press the shutter and when to let something pass; when to push a subject and when to let up; when to orchestrate a picture and when to remain invisible.

I still love being at the center of what is happening in the world, taking pictures that people can respond to. I want people to stop and look at my photographs. If they linger over them, I know I've succeeded. I hope my pictures will have an impact as well as some historical value.

I think of photography as history. Very few photographs will hold up on their own fifty or a hundred years from now. Some pictures will explain themselves and will still be dramatic. Some pictures survive artistically, asking nothing except to be looked at. These pictures can stand alone. But most photographs are enhanced by knowledge of the story behind them—especially pictures that illustrate the news. The events that surround the captured moments are important in photojournalism. Many of my pictures are enhanced by the news of the day. If you saw my picture of John Mitchell fifty years from now, you might ask why it was an award-winning photograph. You wouldn't necessarily know that Mitchell had just been acquitted in his Watergate trial. Take the picture out of context and it's just four men having a good time. I hope that fifty years from now the picture will be interesting in the context of history, as a pictorial record of an event on the day that it mattered.

It's an adventure and achievement to record the lives of famous and important people; to get people to relax and let their guard down so I can photograph what they usually keep hidden. I want to give as near honest an impression as I can of what someone was like.

Photography is recording a part of life, from the street to the studio and back again—the people, places, and events that make news around the world. It's important for me to document life, to capture a moment that won't be repeated, to take that one picture worth looking at.

A few weeks before he died in 1964, I photographed Ian Fleming standing on the beach near his home in Oro Cabeso, Jamaica. I was very keen to do the assignment because the James Bond movies were becoming the rage in Britain, and it was a chance to photograph the creator. He told me he was feeling very ill—it was his heart, he said—but he walked along the beach with me. Being an ex-journalist, he knew the value of a story and told me where I could photograph Britain's biggest trade union leader, Frank Cousins, on holiday in Jamaica. This was a bonus. (28 mm)

Thirteen-year-old Cusi Cram is the great-grand-daughter of Lord Beaverbrook, who owned the *Daily Express* when I worked there. Her mother, Lady Jean Campbell, asked me to photograph Cusi, as she wanted to be a model. This photograph was taken for *People* in 1981 after she had signed as the new teen on a television soap. (Hasselblad, 80 mm)

Diana Vreeland, former editor in chief of *Vogue* magazine, sitting on the floor in the studio in 1980. She has a great sense of drama, a style. She doesn't want to be in this world unnoticed. She is always very dramatic and consequently a good subject photographically. (Hasselblad, 150 mm)

Four-month-old 'Baby David," as he is called to insure his privacy, has a rare birth defect called combined immune deficiency, meaning he is defenseless against germs. He must live inside a big plastic bubble tent. The family, who live in Houston, Texas, had agreed to a story for *Life* in 1972. I didn't want to intrude, but I did want to show what the relationship must be like for a mother unable to touch her own child. (50 mm)

American Billy Hayes was sentenced to life imprisonment in Turkey for allegedly trying to smuggle drugs out of the country. On the night he returned home in 1975, sitting down for his first homecooked meal, apple pie and all, he shuddered briefly and said that for a moment he thought he was somewhere else. His parents and sister looked on apprehensively. He later turned the story of his imprisonment and daring escape into a book and film, *Midnight Express*. Without a caption the picture loses meaning, but knowing who he is makes you want to stop and see what the real Billy Hayes looks like. (35 mm)

No picture had been published of the Carters in their private quarters in the White House when I went to photograph Mrs. Carter in 1980. I wanted to show we were on the second floor but still have an informal picture of her. The half-oval windows on the second floor are very photogenic. I asked Mrs. Carter to pick up her one-year-old grandchild, Sarah, daughter of Jack and his wife, Judy. When people have to lift children they do become more informal. (35 mm)

I had been covering the first Mitchell-Stans trial in the Watergate scandal since it began, but on this day had gone to dinner because it didn't look like the jury would have a verdict until the next day. My reporter called and told me the verdict had come in and John Mitchell was now on his way to his hotel room. That was the end of dinner.

Sometimes you literally must outwait the other photographers to get the picture you want. I let the other photographers and the television crews get their pictures and just waited around until they started drifting away. They had taken their pictures and that was that. Mitchell was jubilant because he had won the case. When there were no other photographers or reporters around, he invited me in to the celebration with his lawyers. (First Place, News Documentary Photos, University of Missouri Pictures of the Year, 1974) (35 mm)

When we arrived in Warsaw, Poland, after President Nixon's trip to Russia in 1971, the president worked the crowd. I turned away from the crowd and thought Bob Haldeman and Dwight Chapin looked interest- ing together. Later they both went to jail over the Watergate scandal. I took just one frame of them together. Sometimes a picture later turns out to be more important than you'd ever expected. (24 mm)

Reporters Carl Bernstein and Bob Woodward broke the Watergate story in the *Washington Post* in 1973. Here their pose is a cliché of how reporters should look. (28 mm)

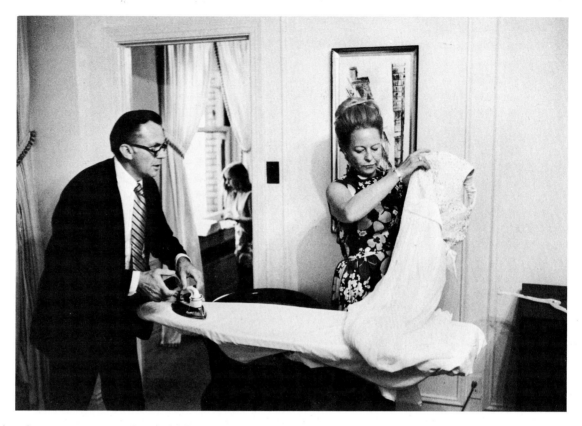

In a St. Louis hotel room in 1970, Martha Mitchell was getting ready to join her husband at the American Bar Association meeting where he was speaking. She was hurriedly ironing her dress with the help of an FBI agent who had been assigned to guard her. Daughter Marty, nine, is at the window. The picture appeared in *Life* and got the FBI agent in trouble because his job was to guard her, not do her ironing. (35 mm)

Congressman Gerald Ford's nomination for vice-president had just been approved by the Senate when I photographed him at his home outside Washington, D.C., in 1973. He liked to get up early, before the rest of his family, fix his own breakfast, read the papers in solitude, and wash his own dishes. (28 mm)

173

As they were about to go onstage at a racetrack in Boston in 1964, I followed the Beatles out of the dressing room and onto the field, photographing them from the back, seeing what they were seeing.

The crowd hadn't noticed them yet; they were just coming out of the shadows. They seemed to be rather apprehensive, a little tense, before the hysteria broke loose. (35 mm)

No book I ever do would be complete without a picture of my children, Wendy and Tessa. I like family album photographs to be candid, unposed. I really dislike family pictures that are set up. Family pictures should record happy moments in the life of a family. They're very personal pictures, pictures just for the family to enjoy. (1981)